FLINT
KNAPPING

FLINT
KNAPPING

A GUIDE TO MAKING YOUR
OWN STONE AGE TOOLKIT

ROBERT TURNER

To my wife, Gillian Turner, who puts up with my flint knapping,
puts up with my writing and then proofreads my work for me.

First published 2013

The History Press
The Mill, Brimscombe Port
Stroud, Gloucestershire, GL5 2QG
www.thehistorypress.co.uk

Reprinted 2015, 2017

British Library Cataloguing in Publication Data.
A catalogue record for this book is available from the British Library.

ISBN 978 0 7524 8874 5

Typesetting and origination by The History Press
Printed in Malta by Melita Press.

CONTENTS

ACKNOWLEDGEMENTS

Especial thanks to:

James Turner, my son, for the photographs in this book; D.C. Waldorf for kind permission to reproduce the drawings of the late Val Waldorf.

My thanks to the following people for help, guidance, contribution and permissions:

Bob Wishoff; Bobby Collins; Brian Thomson; Chris Chitwood; Derek Mclean; Dick Grybush; Ed Thomas; Jack Hemphill; Jerry Marcantel; Kurt Phillips; Larry Kinsella; Mark Ford; Pat Jones; Philip Churchill.

An Introduction to Knapping

I f you have even a passing interest in archaeology then you will soon become acquainted with stone tools. At one time our ancestors made and used these implements on a daily basis to hunt, prepare food and clothing, to farm and make shelters and all the other tasks required for Stone Age existence.

In many parts of the world the most readily available material was flint or chert, which is SiO_2 or silicon dioxide, which is why this art is commonly called 'flint knapping'. Even in igneous rich parts of the world where obsidian, or volcanic glass, is readily available, this terminology can persist.

One of the properties of silicon is that it will carry a shock wave that allows a splitting of the material to be directed along a chosen plane. When you hit a piece of flint, a shock wave travels through the material that causes a fracture along the line of wave. If the impact is sufficiently powerful, this will follow a fairly straight line and parallel the contour of ridges already in the rock. In this way early knappers learned that they could direct the splitting of the rock to achieve a desired shape for severing, cutting and piercing tools.

Flint and chert are what is termed cryptocrystalline, meaning that there is no grain or sheer planes in the rock. The material is sedimentary and was formed in chalk and limestone when these beds were first laid down. Flint which was formed in chalk is varied in colour from white through shades of grey to black, but sometimes it can take on a brown or reddish hue, especially if contaminated by iron. Chert, which is usually a product of limestone, can be a far greater range of colours again dependent on the impurities it acquires. Some of the very best flint can be almost translucent but the rest of the material group is predominantly opaque.

Obsidian, which is an igneous rock formed in volcanic action, can also take on a range of colours. Unfortunately, there is no quality, knappable Obsidian found in Britain, but many other parts of the world, especially the USA, have a range of rhyolites that can take on beautiful banded and coloured forms, which make knapping a wonderful art form.

Many people want to 'have a go' at knapping but because they are unable to know how to start, attempts are usually a disappointing failure. The image of Stone Age man making and using stone tools is one we are all familiar with and as they were our ancestors, there is always a certain amount of attachment to those far-off days. Flint, however, is still all around us, in cigarette lighters and gas and barbeque lighters, all of which carry that small bit of the material. In certain parts of the country flint is a major building material and many of our beaches have shingle, which is just flint by another name.

Go back a hundred and a bit years and gun flints were used all over the world, most of them made in Britain. The gun flint industry was vast and in one year alone, just before the Crimean War, Turkey ordered 11,000,000 flints of various sizes from Britain. Millions were sold to the American and African markets and over a five-year period to 1885 one manufacturer alone, R.J. Snare and Co., produced 23,165,200 gun flints. It is not recorded who counted them but suffice it to say that flint is a material that has been with us since earliest times and still plays a part in our lives today.

Knapping has been carried out for millions of years from the first Hominids through Homo Erectus, Homo Heidelbergensis, and Neanderthals to Homo Sapiens or modern man. In Britain, we date flint tools back almost a million years as 'people' came and went between ice ages. Our modern period started some 10,000 to 12,000 years ago following the end of the Devensian Ice Age and flint tool finds are in profusion, ranging from the Upper Palaeolithic through the Mesolithic, Neolithic and Bronze Age. Especially in the South of England on any fieldwalk you will be able to find worked flint of one sort or another, where flint is common. There is no evidence, currently, of a flint technology in the Iron Age. They may still have used flint tools, we just do not know.

So what are we trying to achieve in these pages? An understanding of how flint was used, the tools that were made and what they were made for, how to make the tools, and detailed instruction of how, with practice, you can replicate the toolkit of your ancestors.

Before we go further, I must make time for the dreaded Health and Safety rules which are totally necessary in knapping. Firstly, flint is sharper than steel and cuts, I am afraid, are a common occurrence. Gloves, or a single glove, are a good idea but thin leather like a golfing glove is far better than the traditional thick gardening type that can inhibit your knapping.

The most important item is eye protection and any form of glasses is a necessity. Your local DIY store will sell a cheap plastic pair of glasses for a few pounds and the outlay is well worth it. Flying bits of flint are rare but do not take the chance. Likewise, when you knap you quickly collect a small pile of shards on the ground around your feet, so do wear suitable shoes. A flint shard will go straight through a thin sole if stepped upon.

Robert Turner, 2013

1

UNDERSTANDING
WHICH ROCKS TO USE

The answer to the question 'what can I knap?' is very simple, it depends where you live. You need to gain some information of the local geology to ascertain if anything around you will be suitable for knapping and the local reference library will provide all you need. Even if you live in an area that is poor in knapping quality rock, your house still has many things that you can practise on.

The easiest things to use are the bottom of a glass bottle, reasonable thick sheet glass (window glass is too thin) and many ceramic materials. The old kitchen sinks that you find in the scrapyards will work quite well, insulators from electric wire carriers and glass and ceramic tiles from your nearest DIY shop can also work. Some of the rocks sold for tropical fish tanks, especially chalcedony (pale blue rock), will knap and all glass-like materials are worth trying.

If you are lucky enough to live in a chalk or limestone area, flint and chert are for the picking up, but many other materials will knap. All you do is get a small sample and fracture it to see if it will take a conchoidal fracture.

Firstly then, we need to understand what a conchoidal fracture is and what it looks like. If you have ever chipped a glass you will have made a conchoidal fracture, as it will have made a small, almost circular or elliptical scar on the glass edge. The word comes from the Greek meaning shell and radiates out from the point of impact in ripples, looking very much like a mussel shell.

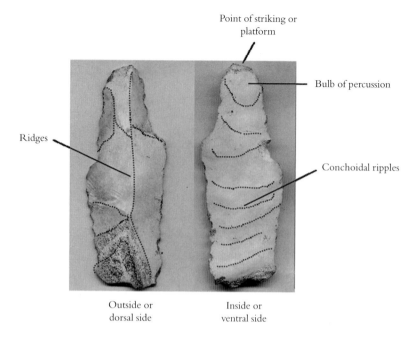

Point of striking or platform

Bulb of percussion

Ridges

Conchoidal ripples

Outside or dorsal side

Inside or ventral side

A conchoidal flake.

What you are seeing is the scar of the shock wave which has a pronounced first wave, called the bulb of percussion, and then a series of smaller waves as the shock progressed through the material. If the rock just breaks with a flat surface, this will not be suitable for knapping, so if you are buying, never invest in a quantity of any material until you have firstly tried it out.

Concentrating on flint, you will also find that lots of nodules are not suitable as they have been on the surface too long and have become impregnated with water, so over the years with successive freezing and thawing they have internally fractured. The thing to do is have a small hammer or a flint pebble and hold up the nodule and then tap it. If it gives a dull thud then this bit is rejected but if it rings it will probably be good, so try to knap off a small section as this will not only tell you if the flint is good but it will also show you the interior of the nodule. This testing will be invaluable as, if you find a flint supply, you can spend time and effort retrieving nodules that are very heavy, only later to find they are useless for knapping.

Flint was laid down in chalk during the last period in the Cretaceous, 85,000,000 to 65,000,000 years ago. The chalk when it was forming (at a rate of about one inch per thousand years) was, on its topmost surface, a mixture of decaying animals and plants. As sea life died it dropped to the undersea surface and rotted away, leaving behind the remnants that will become 98 per cent pure calcium carbonate, the pure white chalk that Dover is famous for.

For those who like the technical details flint is formed as follows ...

During the breakdown of siliceous organisms in the top 5m from sponges, spicules, radiolarian and diatoms we get a deposit of biogenic silica and this supersaturation will precipitate at the oxic-anoxic boundary about 10m down. As the material rots it forms hydrogen sulphide H_2S, the stuff of stink bombs (the rotten egg smell). The H_2S rising within the sediment, from the zone of sulphate reduction, is oxidised to SO_4 and liberates H+ as a by-product. The free H ions lower the pH factor and this results in a calcite dissolution and high concentrate of HCO_3 ions liberated, which act as a seeding agent for precipitation of silica.

The fact that flint forms in bands reflects the cyclic nature of chalk sedimentation and short (in geological terms) pauses halt upward movement of the boundary and encourage flint formation.

Over the aeons the flint nodules will form a crust, called cortex. That requires removal to get to the pristine flint below. As the formation of flint is in a stratum that is also full of animal and plant debris, it can contain fossils and detritus material that affect the shock wave travel when knapping. If, when a flint is struck, it has impurities within it, this will deflect the fracture sideways in what is known as a step fracture. Fissures and flaws will also do this, so the only real way to determine if a flint is sound is to start knapping. Many times you start to work a flint nodule only to discard it after several strikes because you discover impurities or fossils within the flint.

The cortex on the outside of the nodule will absorb energy so it can be difficult to get a flint 'started' when you first strike it. Once you have broken through the cortex, then the knapping becomes much easier.

When flint forms, it is filtrated through the surface material and the further down it sinks in the formation layer the more pure it becomes, so the best flint is always at the bottom of the flint-producing layers. Early man realised this and when mining for flint would dig down through flint layers to get to the best quality. Layers of flint in flint mines are given the terminology of 'top stone', the layer nearest the surface; 'wall stone', intermediate layers; and 'floor stone', the best quality. This is beautifully shown at Grime's Graves, Harrow Hill, Church Hill and many other flint-mining sites.

Very good knappable flint can be recovered from beaches but again test first to decide what is suitable.

Many chalk quarries discard flint as a nuisance when recovering chalk for cement manufacture, but be aware that flint only forms in quantity at the bottom section of the Upper Chalk so not all chalk quarries have flint. Limestone quarries can also have chert suitable for working but take heed that many aggregate quarries may look to have good material but do not have flint or chert of knappable quality. Aggregate deposits are either from ice sheet action or re-deposited by water action so they can be full of flaws – again, a test is required.

Other rocks like dolerite and basalt were used, as was granite, but they do not fracture easily and are very hard to work. Quartz has been used throughout the ages but many of these types of rocks are ground rather than knapped. There are many rocks that are knappable as follows to name a few: calcite, chalcedony, magnesite, jasper, olivine, opal or potch, orthoclase, quartzite, rhodonite, serpentine, sraurolite, onyx, uraninite, zircon and man-made ceramics. Added to this are dozens of rocks that will conchoidal fracture but are very brittle and therefore are not the most suitable choices.

We then come on to the whole group of rhyolites, dacites, novaculites, obsidians and other igneous and metamorphic rocks, some of which can be improved by heat-treating. For further information go online and use your search engine for 'knappable rocks'.

Quality knappable material can be purchased online but it is rather expensive so learn your trade first before investing. It is fair to say that when you start knapping, for a while when you are learning, you will make a considerable amount of gravel. It takes time to become proficient, as you will see further on in this book.

THE CONCHOIDAL FRACTURE
OR HOW KNAPPING WORKS

When you hit your first flint and fracture a flake off the nodule, you hear a sharp crack that sounds different from the noise of just hitting the stone. What you are hearing is the shock wave passing through the flint; it is travelling at several thousand feet a second and it radiates in a Hertzian cone from the point of impact.

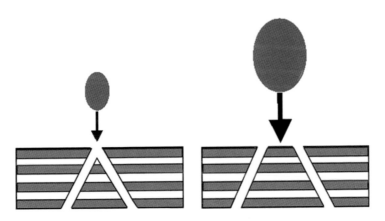

After impact the cone or fracture radiates from the strike point.

Small hammer stone and small impact with a small hammer face produces a pointed cone, while a large stone with an extra large area of impact produces a wide flattenend cone.

Fracture or Hertzian cone.

The wave as it commences its travel performs a diminishing sinusoidal curve with the biggest wave first.

The way the shock wave passes through the flint

This is why you get a series of ripples because the shock wave is travelling in a sinusoidal wave form

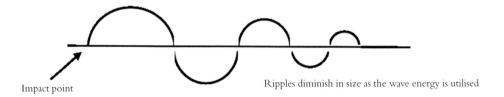

Impact point

Ripples diminish in size as the wave energy is utilised

Sinusoidal wave.

This means that when you look at the flake you have driven off, just below the place you struck, which is called the platform, there is a distinctive bulge called the bulb of percussion. The first time you strike a flake, take a close look at it and you will see at the top, the scar where you hit the flint, lower down the bulb of percussion and then a series of smaller ripples running parallel to the bulb. Sometimes the continuing ripples are not so easy to see but by running your finger down the inside of the flake you can usually feel them. Also quite often you get smaller flake scars on the bulb itself where tiny flakes have been shattered off.

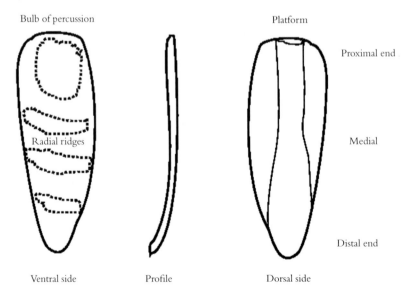

Bulb of percussion

Platform

Proximal end

Radial ridges

Medial

Distal end

Ventral side   Profile   Dorsal side

Flake.

In order to be able to describe flakes, there is a set terminology that should be adhered to. The platform end of the flake, where it was struck, is called the 'proximal' end and the termination or feathered end is called the 'distal' end. Feathering is where a flake gets thinner and thinner until it terminates. The middle part of the flake is called the 'medial' portion. The outside of the flake, the bit you could see before you struck the flake, is the 'dorsal' side and the inner face, revealed by knapping, is the 'ventral' side. Lastly, if the flake is seen edge-on this is the 'profile'.

To remove your first flake you require a 'hammer stone', a pebble about fist size and as round as possible. A beach pebble is great but if you live in an area without pebbles, your local garden centre usually have bins of them. Literally any smooth, round, hard rock will suffice.

Using a knee pad (a bit of carpet works well) hold the hammer stone in your dominant hand, hold the lump of flint on your knee with the other hand and strike with some force near the edge of the flint. Your first attempts can be a bit of a disappointment because this is one of those skills that always looks easier than it actually is, but do not give up because you need to get some experience at just hitting flint. Keep practising until you can remove a flake every time you strike. It does not matter that all you will do is turn big bits of flint into small bits of flint; you are learning a considerable amount even if you do not think you are getting very far.

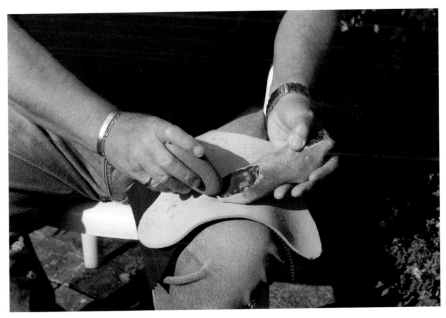

Shown for a right-handed person, ensure that the workpiece is held completely still and with the correct orientation to allow the shock wave to proceed in the desired direction. When you strike, the striking arm must not be allowed to flex, thereby elongating the arc of the strike. To assist in this, the arm is in contact with the body.

When you have removed your first flake, have a close look at the lump of flint where the flake came off. This, to give it its proper title, is now your core. You will find there is a negative bulb on the flake scar that has left a tiny overhang where you struck the core. If you are taking off delicate flakes, it is quite possible that this overhang could affect further flakes being removed from the same place. This lip therefore has to be ground off before you knap again.

Go back to your flake and look at the termination or distal end. If it tapers off to a sharp cutting edge then you have your first success. If it stops with a square abrupt end this is called a 'step fracture', which means that you have hit a flaw or an impurity in the flint and, finally, if you have a rolled termination this is a 'hinge fracture', which is caused by insufficient power in the strike.

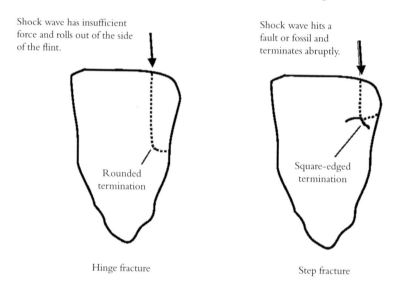

Shock wave has insufficient force and rolls out of the side of the flint.

Shock wave hits a fault or fossil and terminates abruptly.

Rounded termination

Square-edged termination

Hinge fracture

Step fracture

Hinge and step fractures.

You get hinges or steps when something interrupts the shock wave, or if it does not have sufficient power to complete its proper journey; then the shock wave seeks the avenue of least resistance and exits the easiest way it can find from the flint, which is usually sideways to the path of the strike.

By now you will have a sizeable pile of bits or flakes you have struck off your nodules, all of which are extremely sharp, so we need to consider what to do with this waste material that is termed 'debitage'. You must always clear up after a knapping session as children and animals could be stepping on your waste material, so be a responsible knapper. Debitage makes wonderful hardcore for concrete paths and foundations and your local council tip will have a hardcore area. You can put it back in the sea, if it can go somewhere that people do not (remember people are on beaches quite often with bare feet) or you can dig a hole and bury it. This last disposal method has one drawback as your debitage is now indistinguishable from archaeological debitage. A flake is a flake no matter if you struck it or someone struck it 10,000 years ago. It looks the same and flint does not alter with age. It is quite possible that some archaeologist, in say 200 years time, might dig up your cache and think it's from an earlier age. A milk bottle buried with the flint will date it and as glass is as equally long lived as flint there will be fewer problems for future archaeological research.

I wonder how many flint tools in museums are not what they are labelled to be but rather the result of Victorians replicating earlier toolkits. There is just no way of telling.

3

How to Get Started and the Tools you Will Need

We will now go through a detailed step-by-step process of your initial knapping sessions. The first point to make is that knapping is an art that has to be learned, so there is no substitute for practice and you must not be disappointed if you do not get immediate successes. Secondly knapping takes effort and you will get tired, so do not try to knap for extended periods, as inaccuracies will multiply after prolonged and sustained effort.

Do not do a lot of knapping indoors or in confined spaces, as breaking flint causes impact dust and will damage your health if breathed continually. Outdoors is fine but again if it's wintertime, do not get cold, especially if you are concentrating on what you are doing and not noticing your surroundings. Putting down some sort of sheet or tarpaulin to catch the bits is a good idea and many people also have a bucket between their feet, which aids clearing up. This is a good idea, especially if you are knapping on grass, but wherever you knap be sure you clear up.

Let's now turn to equipment. You will need a stool or an upright chair and a small table makes life more comfortable, helping you keep all necessary tools within reach. First on the list is eye protection. If you knap properly flint does not readily fly upwards, but do not take the chance. If you wear glasses they will suffice but if not, your local DIY shop will sell relatively cheap plastic glasses in their tool section for use with power tools. Gloves, or a single glove, are also recommended as the bits that come off are razor sharp but you will find that thick gardening gloves can inhibit your knapping so a thinner glove is better. Having a few sticking plasters around is a good idea but if you are careful serious cuts will not happen. If you do nick a finger the strange thing is that flint cuts do not get infected, but they do become part of the knapping scene as small cuts will happen now and then.

A knee pad is required and for a starter, to save the cost of leather, a piece of old carpet works really well. Cut a square 20cm by 50cm and lay it over your knee with the tufted side down so you are working on the carpet backing.

Wear proper shoes, as the flint pieces or debitage are exceedingly sharp, and sometimes quite pointed, and will go through the sole of a thin shoe. Now you should be ready to start.

Initially it is best to start with hammer stones and we will discuss other ways of knapping as we go along. You need a range of pebbles from about 4cm up to about 10cm or 12cm; these are readily available on pebble beaches or, failing that, your local garden centre will have bins full of them for sale. They need to be as spherical as possible and not have any sharp edges. Lots of materials are suitable as long as they are hard. Flint itself is good and so are granites and most igneous rocks. You can break hammer stones so it is sensible to have a couple of each size. Which size hammer stone you use is entirely dependent on the task. Fine work that does not require a lot of force needs a small tool, while hitting a big flint nodule can take the biggest hammer stone you have.

Range of hammer stones, all as spherical as possible. The bigger the task, the bigger the hammer stone needed; for fine work tiny stones are required. Any hard rock can be suitable but if you do manage to break your hammer stone discard it, as broken edges can cut into your hand as the stone makes contact.

So let's start. If you are right-handed sit comfortably with the hammer stone in your right hand and the pad on your left knee. Hold the material you are trying to knap in your left hand on your left knee as shown overleaf (reverse everything if you are left-handed).

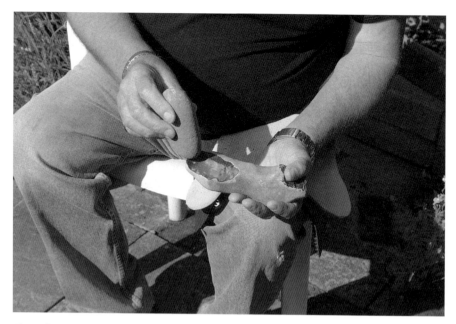

Shown for a right-handed person, this is the standard knapping position. Knap on the left leg just above the knee with a pad sufficiently thick to take any transmitted shock. Orientate the workpiece slightly towards you to allow the best view of the point of contact. The activity of knapping is tiring so make sure that the position is comfortable.

The point where you strike a nodule is called the platform and you must not try to remove a flake if the angle of the face is more than 90 degrees, as the flake will not come off however many times you hit it.

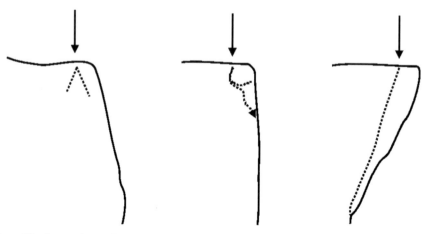

Face of flint is more than 90 degrees – flaking will not occur and all you get is a cone of shock in the flint.

Face of flint is at 90 degrees and will break up and crush.

Face of flint is less than 90 degrees – a successful flake.

A 90-degree face.

If you are working a flint with cortex you will find the first hit harder to accomplish, as cortex can absorb energy. If you strike the nodule a little way into the knapping edge with sufficient force you should remove a flake. If this does not happen then you are either hitting too far into the nodule or not using sufficient strength in your blow. Each time you hit you are making a cone of fracture inside the flint, so repeated hits will only make repeated fractures until the nodule eventually shatters. You have to learn how much force is necessary.

Assuming you have removed your first flake, now turn the nodule over and the flake scar will be the platform for your next strike. You will find this time that the flake removal is easier.

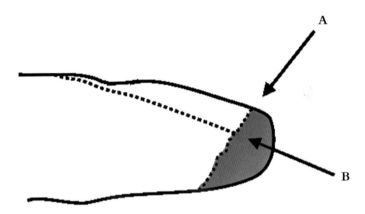

Remove a flake from strike point A, then rotate the flint and remove a flake from position B.

Rotated nodule.

Then it is just repeating the process until you can remove successful flakes every time. This will be quite a good learning process and, although you will only be making bigger bits of flint into smaller bits to start with, you need the experience. A tip is not to start with really good bits of flint, just learn flaking on whatever you can lay your hands on.

The first problem you encounter is that if you make a small pen mark on the nodule and find that you can successfully tap this mark lightly with the hammer stone, when you try to apply force you miss the mark by a wide margin. This is caused by the muscles in your arm lengthening the radius of the strike as you apply it. If you try and pivot the strike from your elbow it will assist, as it is the muscles in your upper arm that are deflecting your blow. Aiming a centimetre short of your mark will also help but this is something you must learn how to do if you want to be successful at knapping. You must be able to hit the spot you are aiming for.

When you have produced your first 20 or 30 flakes take a break and examine the debitage or bits at your feet that you have knocked off. Have a close look at what you have produced and if they are great big chunky flakes then this shows that you are hitting well into your platform, but if you are producing lots of fragments or slivers then this shows that you are hitting too close to the platform edge and crushing it. Your flakes will have four basic characteristics and will be feathered, overshoot, hinged or stepped.

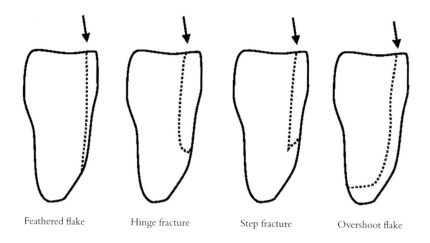

Feathered flake   Hinge fracture   Step fracture   Overshoot flake

The feathered flake is perfectly struck and terminates with smooth distal end; the hinge is when there is insufficient force and the shock wave seeks the easiest avenue of escape sideways; the step is when the shock wave hits a fracture or a flaw; and the overshoot is when too much force is exerted.

If the flake is feathered this is exactly what you are aiming for and shows you are really getting the right idea of how to knap. If it has followed a line round the bottom of the nodule and is thicker at the distal or bottom end then this means that your hit was too strong. If it is hinged or rolled around the end of the flake then this is demonstrating insufficient force, and the shock wave has given up part way through its travel. If the flake terminates in a sharp sideways junction, or breaks into several bits, then this is a fault or imperfections in the flint. So now you can set yourself a target of removing several feathered flakes in a row, but this will take some practice and may take a while to master.

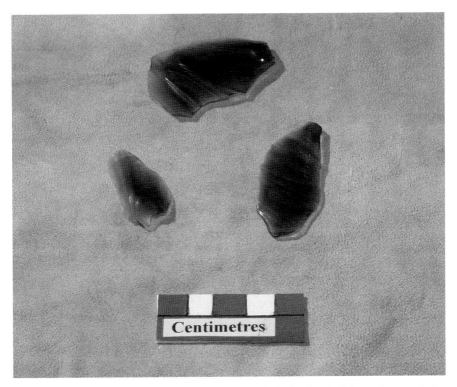

Showing a platform, a bulb of percussion, ripple markings and a feathered end: all the attributes required to demonstrate that the flake was struck by man.

If you rotate the angle of the strike by rotating the nodule on your knee you will find that you can change the length of the flakes; this is because a fine angle will produce long flakes called invasive flakes and an oblique angle will produce short stubby flakes or abrupt flakes.

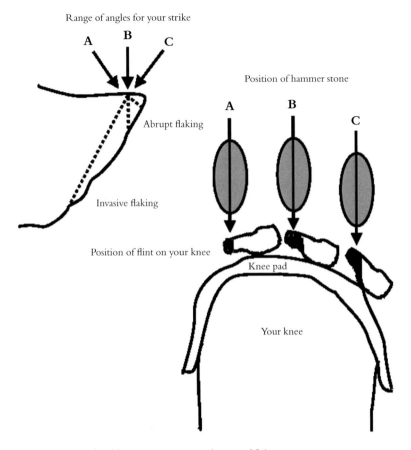

How to position your tool and hammer stone to vary the type of flake.

By now, if you have mastered each step, then you will have accomplished the basics of how to successfully knap flint. If not, there is no short cut to this, so repeat the tasks over again until you can produce the flake you desired.

If you are working from a large nodule of flint, the first process is to reduce it to workable size pieces and this process is called quartering. Although this suggests that you will end up with four pieces this is not so, as the name was derived from gun flint makers and is merely a term for big nodule reduction. Flint that comes from quarries will be all shapes and sizes and therefore an analysis of how to reduce the nodule is essential, so you end up with the shapes you are trying to achieve. Quite often you may have to sacrifice material to achieve your desired result. You will need a sizeable hammer stone for this task and possibly you could use a 4lb club hammer if you cannot get a large enough hammer stone.

As each nodule is unique in its shape there cannot be a standard way of reduction, but hitting into concave depressions will provide suitable pieces for further work.

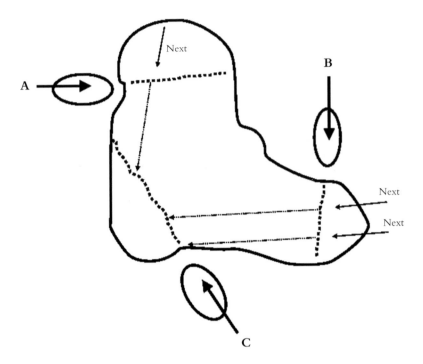

Reduction of a large nodule.

There are two categories of flint tools – 'core' tools and 'flake' tools – and you must decide which you are going to produce before you proceed too far with your quartering. Core tools are when you reduce a nodule down progressively until you achieve the desired shape, while flake tools are produced from flakes and blades taken off a core. The hand axe or biface are good examples of core tools while knives or scrapers are examples of flake tools.

Two hand axes, the shiny one made of dacite and the other basalt, with three scrapers. One of the scrapers is made directly on to a flake and the others are thumbnail scrapers. All three are abruptly retouched on the scraping edge.

For the hand axe a large spall was taken off a nodule and then progressively reduced in thickness by a process called thinning, while the scraper was made by producing a blade core, striking off a blade and then reworking or retouching it. A blade is just a flake that has parallel sides and has a length more than twice its width. From experience, everyone that starts to flint knap seems to want to make a biface initially so let's look at the process.

4

MAKING A HAND AXE

A hand axe is a lenticular-shaped core tool that was used to carry out a number of tasks specific to the hunter who, when grouped round an animal kill, had to butcher the animal as fast as possible, as this was a time of predators and a fresh kill would quickly attract unwanted guests. The first hand axes were required to have a sharp cutting edge but be strong enough to break bone to extract the high protein of bone marrow, so it could render a carcass with all the tasks being done by a single tool.

If you have removed a spall from a large nodule or are working a smaller nodule, the first task is to remove as much of the cortex as is necessary. Total cortex removal is more aesthetically pleasing but not a necessity. If working a smaller nodule, try and select, if you can, a more suitable shape than just any old lump, thinking about the final shape you are trying to achieve. A lenticular-shaped nodule with roughly parallel sides is preferred; rather like the children's sweet, the 'Smarties' shape is desirable. Whatever you select, firstly knock off any parts that are not required and then take a flake from the edge of the nodule. Then reversing the nodule, use the flake scar to remove a further flake and keep reversing and flaking until you have flaked all the way round.

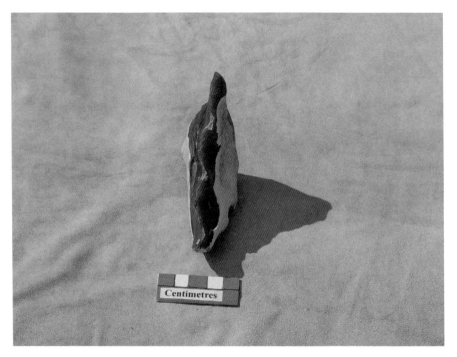

Removing the cortex from a nodule by alternate flaking creates a zigzag edge. Each zig or zag itself then can make a platform for further thinning flakes as they are below the centre line of the workpiece and can be used to initiate further flaking.

When you have achieved a complete circuit the nodule edge-on will have a rough zigzagged edge, so now you have the task of thinning the piece and straightening the edge. Understanding how a knapping process works is crucial at this point as if you do not go about thinning correctly, all that happens is that you keep the same thickness but make your tool smaller. Secondary flakes will follow the lines of previous flakes so you can use this attribute to your advantage. The flakes you require ought to be as long as possible so try and remember the angle of attack. An abrupt angle will produce a short flake, while a flake at a low angle will produce a longer one.

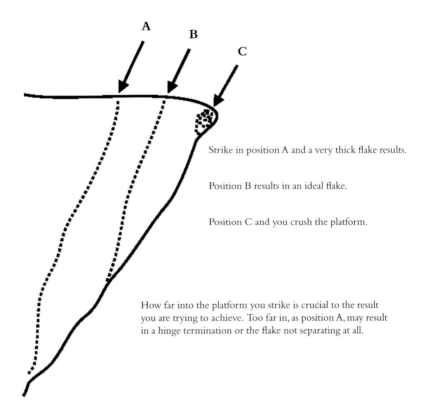

Strike in position A and a very thick flake results.

Position B results in an ideal flake.

Position C and you crush the platform.

How far into the platform you strike is crucial to the result you are trying to achieve. Too far in, as position A, may result in a hinge termination or the flake not separating at all.

Flaking angles.

The process of thinning is sometimes counter-intuitive, where you have to work against what you think you should do, because if you have a thick or triangular cross section, removing flakes from the same side as the last removal will only make the cross section worse. You have to reverse the nodule and create a platform that will allow you to reduce the thickness.

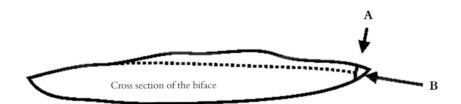

Cross section of the biface

Prepare the platform and strike at a shallow angle so the flake feathers out at least more than halfway across the biface.

Thinning flake.

Thinning is one of the hardest tasks to replicate, as to remove a successful thinning flake you have to hit in the right place with the right force and at the right angle. Until you master this aspect think about what you are trying to achieve. Flakes are to be removed for the sole purpose of eliminating unwanted material, so planning is essential.

You have got to have a platform for the strike, so quite often you have to reverse the nodule and remove an abrupt flake that seems to go against what you are trying to achieve. Once this flake is removed, you can then reverse your rotation and find that you then have a platform that will now allow you to proceed.

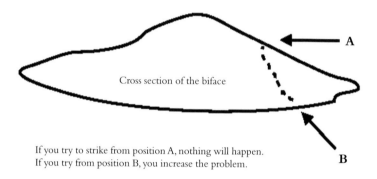

If you try to strike from position A, nothing will happen.
If you try from position B, you increase the problem.

Invert the tool and strike from C to remove the end.
Turn back over and thin from position D.

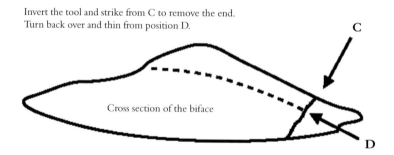

Thinning a roughly triangular cross section rough-out.

Quite often when removing thinning flakes what will happen is that you crush the platform edge. This is because the very edge of the flint is quite weak and the amount of power you put into the strike is utilised in and disbursed in breaking up the edge, so you may have to strengthen the platform. This is done by abrading the edge with a rough pebble or a broken bit of an old grinding wheel. You can be quite rough with the edge of the flint, as what you are trying to do is round it off by getting rid of its fragility. This makes it much stronger and allows the shock wave to pass through the edge rather than breaking it up.

In the archaeological record there are lots of preform shapes for hand axes – some pointed, some rounded and some like the bout-coupé with an indented base.

You will undoubtedly make lots of hand axes before you arrive at a final example that you are really satisfied with. The achievement goes up incrementally as you progress, until you reach the stage where you can actually make the direction of flake removal go exactly where you want it to. There is no quick and easy route to this, you just have to keep on practising.

Also a word about 'end shock' that really is a surprise, as sometimes, as a shock wave travels through a nodule, some strange things can happen. To have a large nodule on your knee and hit one end to have the other end fall off is a strange experience. It is caused by impurities in the material you are working with or stresses if you are working with materials like glass. Be aware that you can spend considerable time making a beautiful tool and towards the end of the manufacture end shock happens and you suddenly have two half tools in your hand.

You will, however, gain tremendous satisfaction from your early attempts once you get the hang of knapping and even if your flint has flaws that you are aware of, other people will not see them. There is almost a mystique about seeing a hand axe being made and people will be very complimentary – usually in your early attempts – once you have mastered the art sufficiently to make it look reasonable. Do not forget your attention has been concentrated on this small object for quite a while so only you know what went wrong in places, which is a great incentive for you to get better and better at the task.

When removing flakes, if you hit with insufficient force then you will get a flake termination just in from the edge of the workpiece and this cannot be removed by taking a further flake from the same place, as all you will do is worsen the fault as a second flake will terminate in the same place. All you can do is try to remove the fault from a different direction or from the other side of the tool.

5

MAKING A BLADE CORE

B lade removal from a core is another facet of knapping that you must acquire to enable you to make a range of tools. To start this process you must prepare a core that is a flat platform with a side at less than 90 degrees.

The perfect core with blades removed from 360 degrees.

One way of achieving this is to split a pebble in half or to remove a bulbous end from a nodule. Quite often, if the basic core is the right shape, you can start removing blades all round but this is not necessarily required, as beautiful blades can be removed from just one side or just a small part of the core. Firstly, however, you will have to remove the cortex and hopefully, if you are accurate enough, you can take these off in parallel stripes down the face of the core.

A blade core in obsidian and a Mousterian core in flint. The blade core is prepared by percussion and then the blades are removed, by pressure flaking, with a large double-handed ishi stick. The flint core is prepared and blades are struck by percussion.

Once you have removed the cortex, then you can begin to remove blades. How easy that sounds! You are in for quite a bit of practice before you can achieve those few words. Platform preparation is essential, as it will determine if you want to remove a crested blade or a double-crested blade, because the shock wave will tend to follow the existing scar crests of the blade taken to remove the cortex.

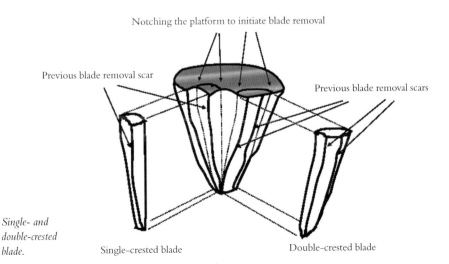

Single- and double-crested blade.

Initially, the platform edge must be removed by abrading as the previous blades. The bulb of percussion will leave a small overhang that will impede the next blade removal. Abrading will also make the platform stronger, as blade removal requires a controlled strike near to the core edge. Sometimes, to get a perfect blade, it becomes necessary to produce an 'isolated platform' where you remove some material from each side of the platform and this will help initiate the shock wave from the correct position.

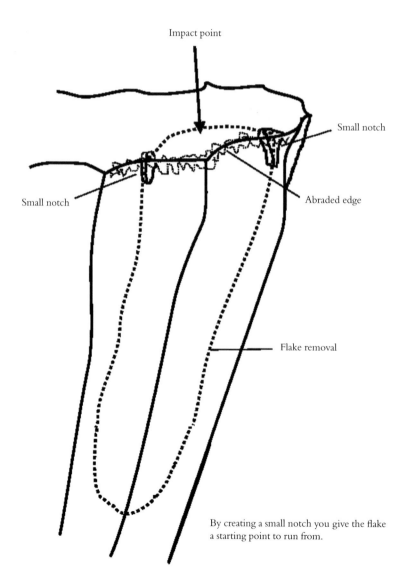

Impact point

Small notch

Small notch

Abraded edge

Flake removal

By creating a small notch you give the flake a starting point to run from.

The isolated platform.

Your blade strike must be at the right angle and with sufficient force, for if you 'under-hit', in force terms, the blade will hinge terminate halfway down the face of the core. If you 'over-hit' this will make your blade take more of the lower part of the core and thicken the blade at its distal end.

If you get a hinge fracture or a step fracture this can only be removed by reversing the core, creating a new platform and taking a blade from the other end of the core. This is then called a bipolar core. Any fault halfway down the blade core cannot be rectified by taking a second blade from the same plat-form as you now have a weakness in the face of the core and the next shock wave will follow the same line.

The art of removing blade after blade is something special and will only be achieved with considerable practice. Once again there is no short cut. You must prepare the platform for every blade and each removal must leave the scars for a further removal. Cores can, if worked well, produce dozens of blades, all of which will be utilised in further tool production.

By this stage you will have become a useful knapper, able to produce a basic core tool and make blades. So before we proceed to the production of a range of tools, let's look at the history of knapping and the full range of tools that were produced throughout the ages.

6

THE HISTORY OF KNAPPING

This chapter takes a look at the tools from the Palaeolithic, the Mesolithic, the Neolithic and the Bronze Age and relatively modern flint production from the 'New World'.

From archaeological evidence we appear to have had 'people' living in the British Isles for the best part of one million years and, although through the last seven ice ages the land has only been habitable for about 30 per cent of the time, we still have a rich heritage of knapping. Tool production from Homo Habilis, Homo Erectus, Homo Heidelbergensis, Neanderthalis and Homo Sapiens have all been found from one source or another. This book is not intended to contribute to archaeological investigation of early man but to try and show how the tools were created and to explain how they were made in date order.

At all stages our ancestors used the local available rock and although there is some evidence of trade of finished or rough-out materials, mostly people used what they could find, so we have a wealth of different rocks from sedimentary through metamorphic to igneous to look at. Obviously, where areas were only supplied with the granite type rocks there was grinding and pecking processes at work, but where flint was readily available, like the south and west of England, knapping was in full flourish.

The first Hominids to use flint discovered that if you break open a nodule you get a sharp edge that can be used for cutting and scraping, so the very earliest tools are quite difficult to recognise. The tools were difficult to distinguish between naturally fractured accidents of nature and deliberately made tools. Indeed, naturally fractured stones must have been the earliest used tools. These first 'man-made' tools were termed 'Eoliths' and require little skill to manufacture. They are often undistinguishable from Nature's work in heating and freezing rocks and producing equally sharp edges and points.

The very first deliberately 'man-made' tools of the Lower Palaeolithic were choppers and proto axes, but the act of manufacture of these tools produced flakes and blades that were in turn used, so the two basic types of tools, core and flake, were created simultaneously.

To produce a simple chopper, take a pebble and strike a flake. Reversing the tool, take two more flakes from each side using the edge of the first flake as a platform and you can produce a serviceable working sharp tool. The three flakes that were removed are sharp knives that are instantly useable. If you do this on a bigger rock, you have a lethal heavy tool that can break any bone in any kill or scavenged prey and produce knives to cut and trim skin as well.

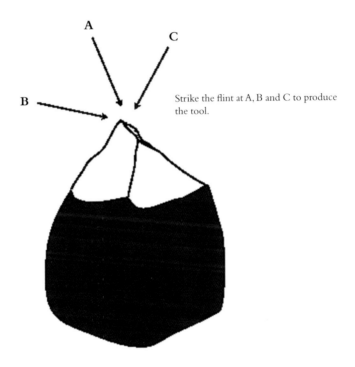

Strike the flint at A, B and C to produce the tool.

A simple point and chopper.

Repeat the process but this time, take a big initial flake and a series of secondary flakes and you have a serrated edge or a chopping edge. These tools are fun and easy to make and help in your learning of knapping skills. Termed 'Oldowan', these tools retained most of their cortex and were later refined with abrupt retouch on the flake scar to form a steep scraping edge that added a different use to the tool. To produce a scraping edge to a tool or a flake, hit into the edge at an acute angle with a series of small blows equally spaced. If you are doing this on a flake, it may be a requirement to firstly trim up the shape of the flake.

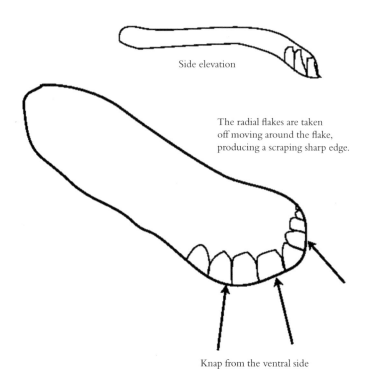

Side elevation

The radial flakes are taken
off moving around the flake,
producing a scraping sharp edge.

Knap from the ventral side

Flaking technique and a scraper.

For a far more detailed look at flint types and flint usage, Chris Butler has produced an excellent book, *Prehistoric Flintwork,* that should be read in conjunction with this work to obtain the broader picture of prehistoric tools and their periods.

Later core tools began to be refined into a number of different forms to enable different tasks to be performed. The rough-out stage was still done with hammer stones to remove most of the unwanted material but the use of antler hammers (also known as soft hammers) allowed a more refined structure to be carried out. Hand axes came in all sizes from 8cm in the longitudinal axis up to at least one known ficron type that measured 33cm from proximal to distal ends.

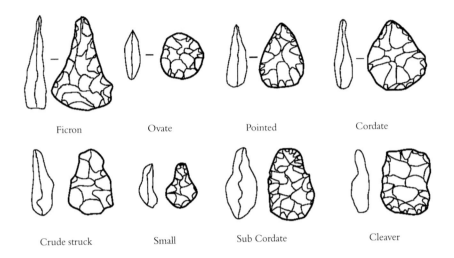

Ficron   Ovate   Pointed   Cordate

Crude struck   Small   Sub Cordate   Cleaver

Selection of various types of hand axes.

The profile of axes ranged from pointed distal ends to heart-shaped or cordate axes to ovates that were elliptical and the waist-shaped ficrons. The principle of manufacture was virtually the same, with the knapper selecting the shape detail as thinning progressed. For most axes, save the ovate, the thickness lessens as you approach the distal end, though some of the axes that had to carry out the heaviest tasks were quite weighty with the amount of material incorporated. The ovate was biconvex, with only a very small narrowing at the lesser diameter end.

The thinning method utilised the zigzag shape from the first pass of flake removal by striking in the lower part of each zig or zag, thus bringing the cutting edge into line. The final flaking was usually to sharpen the final edge and in the case of cordates and ovates, this was often by the removal of a tranchet flake that removed a transverse flake that ran laterally across the axe, so producing a very sharp edge.

Four axe-sharpening flakes found from the raised beach extension at the Valdoe bottom, West Sussex. Found just below the Fe/Mg layer and dated at 485,000 BP, this was the work of Heidelbergensis. (Reproduced by kind permission of Pat Jones)

Stage 1
Select a rounded nodule and remove flaking 360 degrees.

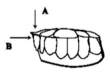

Stage 4
Abrade and strengthen the platform A. Strike off the Levallois flake B.

Levallois reduction.

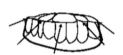

Stage 2
Flake using the previous flake scars and turn into a dome or turtle-back shape.

The Levallois flake.

The remaining cone.

Stage 3
Prepare a platform for the removal of the Levallois flake.

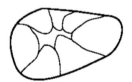

The dorsal side of the Levallois flake will have radial flaking, while the ventral side will have the bulb of percussion.

The photograph opposite shows axe-sharpening flakes found at the Boxgrove raised beach continuation dated circa 485,000 years ago that were recovered as sharp and fresh as the day they were struck.

As the Palaeolithic period developed, a new method of biface production came into being, that of the Levallois reduction, which produced a much thinner biconvex shape. This was achieved by taking radial flakes from a preformed nodule and then removing the end to produce a platform where the whole flake can be taken off.

The Levallois blank is easily recognised by the radial flaking on the ventral side and the large bulb of percussion on the dorsal side. Quite often the Levallois flake was then reworked to smooth out the bulb of percussion and to sharpen the edges. This reworking sometimes disguises the original Levallois reduction. To produce a Levallois blank, take your nodule and trim all unwanted parts off so radial flaking can occur. Flake through 360 degrees and this will produce a turtle-shaped ventral side. The end is now decapitated and this makes a platform to allow the top of the turtle shape to be removed in one hit and will form a roughly oval shape. The main idea of this process was to make a thinner flattened shape without a long process of thinning.

Every knapper should attempt the Levallois reduction and it is best to start with a nodule that is roughly lenticular. Begin with a reasonable-sized hammer stone and take a flake off the nodule extending as far into the middle of the workpiece as possible. From the same side of the nodule take a flake next to the one previously removed and then following that another, moving around a full 360 degrees until you meet up with the first flake. It is aesthetically pleasing to remove all cortex so if there is any remaining on the lower side of the tool it may well be a requirement to carry on knapping from the same side, this time utilising the ridge scars from the first pass. If you are knapping correctly the second pass will produce longer flakes, as they will follow the scars already produced by knapping.

Once you have achieved the removal of all cortex, reverse the tool and you should be faced with a dorsal side covered in radial flake scars. You now have to create the platform for the removal of this face and a strong platform will be required so remove an abrupt flake from this side, hitting at least a centimetre into the face at an upright angle so the flake leaves a platform about 60 to 80 degrees.

Abrade this edge quite heavily and then with a weighty hammer and lots of force strike well into this platform and you should remove a substantial flake that is roughly circular across most of the prepared dorsal surface, as shown in the Levallois reduction diagram opposite. The flake is biconvex and may well have a sizeable bulb of percussion that can be trimmed up, using a smaller hammer or abrading stone, to produce a symmetric face. There is a further Levallois reduction that can be used where you produce a core with a central ridge, and by creating a platform at the end of the ridge you can remove a 'point' in one strike. This allows further removals and a working point is produced from the previous removal scar.

Stage 1
Prepare a core with a central
ridge by taking parallel flakes off.

Stage 2
Prepare the end as a platform.

Stage 3
Strike consecutive flakes.

The residual core.

Further flakes can be removed
until the core is exhausted.

The first flake removed is
a point with a continuous
ridge on its dorsal side.

The second flake
removed is a fluted,
finished point.

Each removal will produce
a larger point as you work
along the central crest.

Levallois point, subsequent point and final product.

Up to now we have only discussed the use of hammer stones for flint work
but, as we need more delicate flaking, now may be a good time to discuss 'soft
hammers'. This term is given to anything that is used for striking to remove
flakes that is softer than stone. The most common soft hammer is antler and a
whole range of sizes can be obtained from the various types of deer that we
find in the British Isles. Roe and fallow deer have relatively small antlers leading up to red deer with the largest.

   Where an antler joins the skull there is a crown and it is this part of the
antler and main body up to the first branch that can make a suitable hammer.

*Antlers from red deer,
roe deer and fallow deer
can all be used and give
tools of varying sizes and
thicknesses. The crown
where the antler was
attached will make a soft
hammer and the tines
pressure flakers.*

Antler can be sawn quite readily with a hacksaw and a rough file will remove sharp edges and the outside of the crown. If the lower part of the antler is used make sure that, especially with smaller deer, you have the correct antler as they twist to the left and right dependent on which side of the deer's head they came from. You may find that if you have hammers from each side, one will require more filing than the other to produce the right shape for you to use. Do not discard the remainder of the antler as many other parts can be turned into tools, as we will show in later chapters.

The antler is sawn off 10cm to 15cm above the crown and then the crown itself filed away to produce a hammer end. The large hammer is red deer and the smaller is roe deer. With roe or fallow deer the antlers are handed (curved for the left or the right, depending on the use) so the hammer handle will be twisted. For right-handed people it is better to have a right-side antler.

Antlers are readily obtainable from a number of sources, deer farms, stately homes, butchers, abattoirs and the Internet; in fact anywhere there are deer, because do not forget that after each mating season male deer shed their antlers and will produce many pairs during their lifetime.

The hard woods and some of the high impact plastics will also make soft hammers, so there is a range of materials you can use. The idea of a soft hammer is that it can produce flakes with smaller bulbs of percussion and carry out more delicate strikes, so it is suitable for finishing and sharpening flint tools.

Returning to the Levallios reduction, a soft hammer can now be used to trim up your tools and by taking smaller, shallower flakes can straighten the cutting edge and give a sharper form.

By the Middle Palaeolithic, a series of tools were in evidence based on blade and flake removal from cores. Scrapers of several varieties including end, side and hollow types, denticulates, burins and knives, and especially the notched piece that was produced on the edge of flakes.

To understand these tools we must introduce the concepts of retouch and pressure flaking. Retouch is where a flake or blade has been modified along one, or more than one, edge. This modification can be by knapping with a smaller hammer or by the use of different types of tool that utilise pressure exerted rather than a strike. Pressure flaking is carried out by pushing a tool against the edge of the workpiece and gradually increasing pressure until the flint gives way and a conchoidal flake is detached.

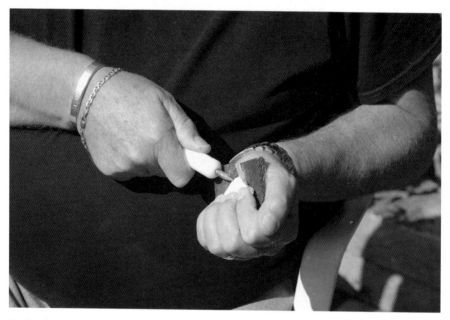

For hand pressure flaking you are relying simply on upper-body strength, so do not try and remove too much material at one go. The line of pressure is through the pressure flaker and towards the knuckle of your index finger. Do not allow the wrist to collapse as this will alter the line of pressure. The flaker is grasped firmly with the index finger tucked out of the way if the flaker slips.

Small flakes can be removed with upper-body or arm pressure but if more force is required, your leg muscles can be brought into play.

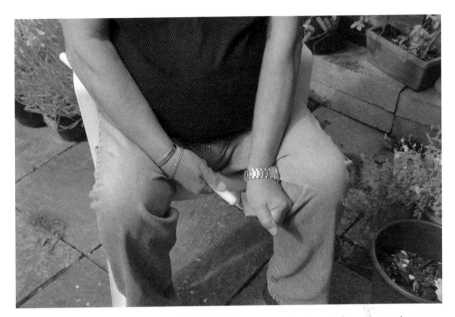

This is one of the hardest positions to get right. The aim is to use your legs to exert the pressure as they are many times stronger than just upper-body strength. Both hands are in contact with the legs and the movement is to close the legs using your thigh muscles to force the pressure flaking to work. The effort you can exert with your legs is quite surprising as the line of force is again directed toward the knuckle of the index finger. The pressure pad is held parallel to the ground and the pressure flaker at the same angle as when it was hand-held. If the pressure pad is not horizontal, short flakes will occur as the angle of attack will change.

If pressure flaking is carried out then you must have the protection of a pad or block should the flaking tool slip after doing its work, so, if it carries on its path of trajectory and comes into contact with your hand or the inside of your leg, you are protected. For hand flaking, a piece of leather is adequate or a small solid pad, while if you use leg muscles for greater pressure then the notched pad is a desirable choice.

A platform is still required so that the flaking tool has something to bite in to and the path of the pressure is the same as flaking when striking, as longer flakes will require a more acute angle of attack.

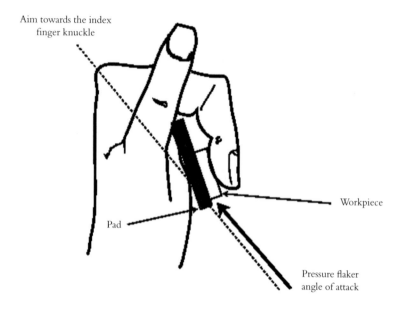

Aim towards the index
finger knuckle

Workpiece

Pad

Pressure flaker
angle of attack

Correct angle for pressure flaking.

The angle of pressure is aimed at the first joint of the first finger holding the flake to be modified that will create an elongated retouch flake on the inside of the workpiece. For the making of the blade and flake tools there should be an awareness not only of what the tools looked like but also their usage.

End scraper

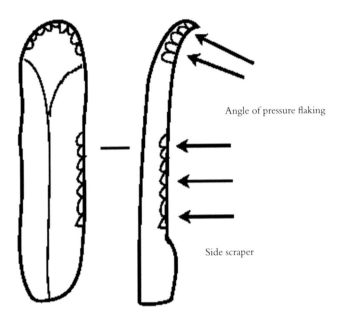

Angle of pressure flaking

Side scraper

End scraper and side scraper.

The scraper provided the ability to remove unwanted fat from animal skins and could be made on a flake or a blade, provided the piece was thick enough. Sort through your debitage for a thick flake and, working from the inward side of the curve, take a series of small flakes either by percussion or by pressure flaking. The same can be done on a thick blade working on the end or on the side. The aim of a scraper is to produce a sharp but oblique edge so you can scrape but not cut into the material you are working on. More will be said about scrapers in future chapters but for now the ability to make a scraper is not difficult, however, do try and test your finished product.

Using a sharpened pressure flaker and working from the ventral side, take a series of small nicks from the flake edge.

The result is an exceedingly sharp saw.

Making a denticulate from a flake.

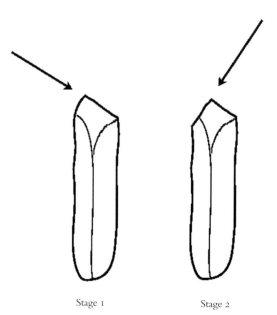

Stage 1

Remove a spall at 45 degrees to the centre line of the flake.

Stage 2

Remove a second spall to give a resultant corner of 90 degrees.

Making a dihedral burin on a flake.

With a sharpened antler tip or a thick blade it is possible to work along a sharp-edged blade and remove small nicks or notches. This produces a saw-like structure that will cut through wood quite easily and is a 'denticulate'.

The burin or graver is a tool found through much of the flint tool calendar and its usage has been the subject of much speculation. It is obviously a specialist type of cutting tool but as little remains to us from these far off times, save the flint tools themselves, it is difficult to say exactly what its usage was. A flake was modified by removing spalls from the end (as shown) and this leaves an abruptly pointed end. Experiments have been carried out that show a burin can be used to manufacture the serrated edges of denticulates.

Stage 1

Remove a notch from
the side of the flake.

Stage 2

Working from the ventral side
with a sharp pressure flaker, take
a series of small notches as when
making a scraper.

Making a notched blade from a flake.

This is frequently made on a backed knife; the sharp blade end is abraded to form a platform and then a notch is made by a single strike into the platform. Working in exactly the same way as a scraper, a tool of this nature would be used for bark removal or processing or smoothing wooden shafts.

By the Upper Palaeolithic, a whole range of tools emerged that show a technical improvement on toolkits of previous eons. A very distinctive tool was the long leaf-shaped point.

Leaf-shaped arrowhead, sometimes called a laurel leaf.

These points were made from an elongated, triangular-shaped blade and had invasive retouch quite often over both ventral and distal faces. Between 10cm and 15cm long and pointed at the distal end, the blade was abraded down both edges to make platforms and then pressure flaked, with some flakes crossing the entire face of the piece. Sometimes the proximal end was reworked to make a tang. The other tool that was common in this period was the piercer, which was retouched to produce a piercing point on the tool.

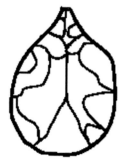

Piercers made on flakes. The size of the sharpened end determines the size of hole that can be made.

The people of this and subsequent periods were opportunists and would carefully examine flakes in the knapping process as, occasionally, a flake will naturally come off a nodule with a piercer shape, and it takes very little abrupt retouch to enhance the tip to make the piercing tool.

In Britain, the last inhabitants before the Devensian Ice Age reached its maximum were living circa 35,000 to 40,000 years ago and from then on we were in the grip of an ice sheet that stretched roughly from the Bristol Channel to the Thames, with southern Britain being a polar desert. The ice maximum was some 28,000 to 18,000 years ago and then the ice grip gradually receded. The last phase of the Palaeolithic was from about 12,500 BP. In the northern part of the Atlantic there was a brief hitch in the relenting of the ice called the Younger Dryas. It was caused by the melt waters from the Laurentian Shield not being able to find sufficient outlet in America's great river systems and formed the Great Lakes. This sudden outburst of fresh, cold water from what is now Canada changed the salinity of the Atlantic and for a time altered the Gulf Stream, which made Britain colder for a short period.

This last part of the Palaeolithic, Late Upper and Final Upper has left very few finds in Britain, but those that have been discovered show a refinement of scrapers, burins, blades and shouldered and tanged points, but also we see the beginning of the technology that produced microliths.

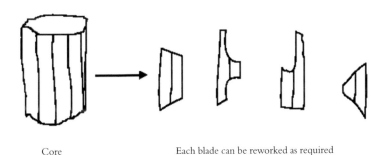

Core   Each blade can be reworked as required

Microliths.

Few of these composite tool pieces are found in British archaeology from this time due to lack of inhabitants, but this was the forerunner of things to come.

The Mesolithic Period

Between 10,000 BP and 9,500 BP Britain underwent a great change as the temperatures rose and woodland returned, followed by animals and the incursions of hunters. This part of the world was still a peninsular of Europe and because the main rivers – the Seine, Thames and Rhine – were combined in a great river flowing down to what is now the English Channel, entry into Britain was across the North Sea in what was then Doggerland.

This was the time of the blade and blade core, made of the finest flint for the production of microliths and micro tools. Many cores from this period are bipolar or worked from both ends to produce the blades or bladelets needed for production of multi-use tools. There are numerous types of microlith but their production required thin blades that could firstly be notched and then broken before retouching and mounting to make composite tools. Some microliths were snapped off from bladelets without notching first being carried out, but these are in the minority.

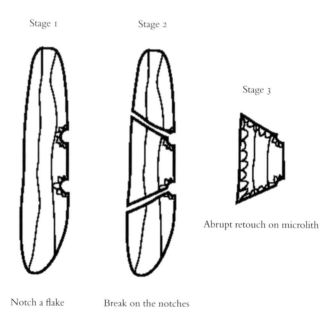

Stage 1   Stage 2

Stage 3

Abrupt retouch on microlith

Notch a flake   Break on the notches

Microlith production.

Microliths come in all shapes and sizes with point or flat ends, lozenge-shaped, rounded, square, triangular and chisel ended. Each shape may have been for a different task and different tools such as spears, arrows, fishing tools and in later periods knives and sickles. Each was retouched with tiny working along one or several edges. Several different attempts have been made to classify or group microliths by type and again for further reference I would draw your attention to published works on the subject.

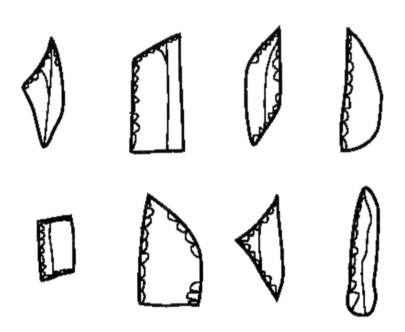

Several types of microlith.

The diagram above shows a few of the types of microliths, each with its distinctive shape. Again the pressure flaking tools were very delicate and it's likely that a flint was used as a pressure flaking tool, as antler may well have been too cumbersome for such delicate work.

The Mesolithic was also the time of the adze, often referred to as a tranchet adze, and picks that were quite crudely made and exceedingly robust, as they were required to carry out heavy tasks. Axes were also present and all three were robust core tools firstly preformed on site and then finished and sharpened at a later stage. These tools can be up to 30cm to 35cm in overall length although small versions, under 10cm, have been found.

Pick

Usually crudely made with
a roughly pointed end.

Axe

Well made with a sharpened
and tapered end; could be a
rough-out for polishing.

Adze

More crudely made with
a tranchet flaked end.

Adze, axe and pick.

Some smaller adzes were made from large flakes but mainly they were core
tools and were probably hafted. Sharpening was by removal of a lateral or
tranchet flake rather than a series of small sharpening flakes as in the hand
axe. Many tranchet flakes have been found showing that the tools were re-
sharpened many times. Obviously many of these core tools were made from
suitably-shaped flints and in lots of cases the cortex still remains in areas from
the knapping process.

It must be borne in mind that many of the tools from this and later periods were manufactured, used and then discarded. Blades and scrapers would
take time to re-sharpen so it was easier to discard the worn tool and make a
new one. Cores, on the other hand, were curated as they were the source for
further tools.

From all periods there were obviously beautifully made items that may have
had some ritualistic purpose, but in the main these tools were a tiny minority.

Another tool that was found from the Mesolithic was the fabricator, which
has been the subject of much speculation as to its use. They were finely made
and appear to have been curated and may well have been pressure flaking
tools. Over the periods of time they changed in shape and can be triangular,
oval, circular or diamond-shaped in cross section but all are rod-shaped with
rounded, pointed or beak-shaped ends. Fabricators are generally found well
worn so they must have been in constant use. Many were made from crested
blades where the core was trimmed both sides of the crested blade to give a
shape like the prow of a ship. The flake was then struck well into the platform
to give a thick flake.

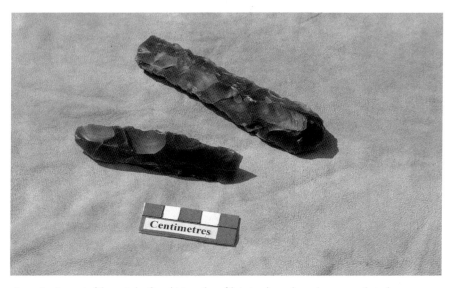

Appearing in most of the periods of pre-history, these fabricators have always been somewhat of a mystery. Their use is not fully understood but they are often worn, indicating use, and the numbers found would appear to show that they were curated. There is some evidence to show that they were used as pressure flakers.

After removal from the core the 'rods', as they are sometimes called, were then flaked on many of their surfaces. Different shaped tips were obviously intended for different uses but experimentation shows that they can be used for pressure flaking and perform extremely well.

Awls and drills were basically the same shape as piercers except that the tip, in the case of an awl, has abrupt retouch along one side or alternate sides and the piercer that is retouched on two lateral sides. Drills have retouch along both edges of a small blade extending away from the tip.

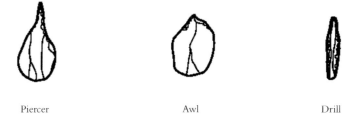

Piercer

Awl

Drill

Piercers have abrupt retouch on both internal sides to give a triangular cross section.

Awls are retouched along one side or alternate edges.

Often called mèches de foret, drills are retouched along both sides to give a lanceolate shape with a point at each end.

Piercer, awl and drill.

The Neolithic Period

Neolithic or New Stone Age covers the period when the hunter-gatherer starts to become a farmer. Do not, however, think that this was an overnight happening as it was a slow transition and many of the tools made for the Mesolithic continued into the Neolithic. Scrapers, blades, piercers etc. were in evidence and some ninety different tool types have been recorded.

This period saw the advent of the leaf-shaped arrowhead that was manu-factured from a flake and invasively retouched, quite often, on both sides by pressure flaking to form a laurel leaf shape. Sometimes the arrowhead was pointed at both ends and sometimes rounded on the proximal end that was attached to the arrow shaft. Normally they were beautifully made, with great care taken in the thinning and pressure flaking.

Ogival form   Leaf form   Kite form

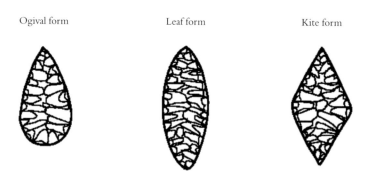

Neolithic types of laurel leaf-shaped arrowheads.

Blades still formed a great part of life but the advent of the longer serrated blade, usually on a backed knife, became common, as different tasks required different tools.

To make this tool you need to take a sizeable flake from the edge of a core, retaining the cortex on the back edge, and then pressure flake small or tiny notches along the length of the blade edge. The size of the serration on the blade will be dependent on the tool use, with large 'teeth' for heavier tasks.

On a backed blade, indent the sharp edge with a series of notches to produce a saw-like appearance.

Serrated knife.

Composite sickles were made from a number of small blades or flakes mounted into a groove on a wooden shaft; the blades or flakes were like microliths but of a larger size. Sometimes the cortex was retained on the back edge and sometimes the blades were denticulated.

Y-shaped scrapers started to appear and are very distinctive with the points of the 'Y' often being worked.

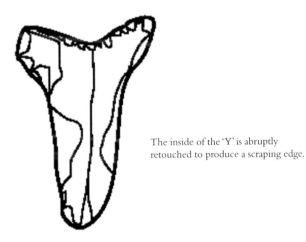

The inside of the 'Y' is abruptly retouched to produce a scraping edge.

A 'Y' scraper.

This period marked the transition from seasonal camps of hunter-gatherers to more settled farming communities. Monuments were built like Causeway Enclosures and long barrows that indicated permanency of land occupation. The toolkit therefore changed accordingly with the different needs of the people and one of the main manifestations was the development of the adze.

We will use the manufacturing of an axe as an exercise in flint knapping in a later chapter, following the way in which Neolithic man made this tool. The site of raw material provided the nodules that were then roughed out for transportation, as there was little use in transporting unwanted material. The axe was then 'preformed', that is to say a final removal of cortex and a general shaping up and then the finishing stage.

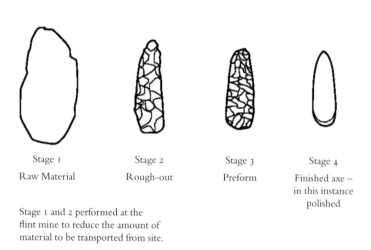

Stage 1   Stage 2   Stage 3   Stage 4

Raw Material   Rough-out   Preform   Finished axe –
                                                                        in this instance
                                                                        polished

Stage 1 and 2 performed at the
flint mine to reduce the amount of
material to be transported from site.

Stages of axe manufacture.

The requirement of large nodules of flint of good quality promoted the development of mining to extract the lowest level of flint called 'floor stone', which was the best quality. Grime's Graves in Norfolk and Cissbury Hill, Harrow Hill, Blackpatch and Church Hill in Sussex are some of the best examples of these mining sites.

The Bronze Age

This was the time of the introduction of the first metals and some tools such as daggers were replicated in flint as metal was not obtainable and so was highly prized and therefore a 'rich man's' possession. Many of the tools in the late Neolithic and early Bronze Age were beautifully made, suggesting specialised flint knappers, but as the period progressed and metals became more readily available the flint craftsmanship deteriorated and by the end of the Bronze Age flint tools were a very crude and utilitarian affair.

Daggers were especially cared for and time and effort to replicate their metal counterparts is astounding. Some of the examples from Denmark are so finely made that they show replicated stitching on the handles. The dagger in Europe developed in this period from a plain elongated bifacial struck blade to the metal original with a square or diamond-shaped handle.

Type 4 dagger drawn by the author.

Barbed and tanged arrowheads were again manufactured with great skill and precision, and some are so thin it is questionable as to whether they would have stood up to use as an arrow. Many are found pristine as they may have formed some ritual usage, or perhaps were used as barter currency.

Barbed and tanged arrowheads from the Late Neolithic and Early Bronze Age (Beaker period).

Discoidal knives are found in the Bronze Age and these were manufactured from a discoidal core and then bifacially worked to produce a sharp edge. Quite often discoidal knives were ground and polished to finish the process and the thinking is that these were combination tools put to several uses.

If you take a roughly circular core or nodule, a coin-shaped disc can be removed by inverting the core and striking as a core rejuvenation flake. The strike is about a centimetre in from the face and with practice the flake can have almost parallel ventral and dorsal sides.

By the end of the period and the start of the Iron Age, the use of flint became less common as metals became available in greater quantities. With this trend the care in production deteriorated, with rough tools made from virtually any piece of flint including thermal flakes.

In the history of knapping it only remains to mention the production of gun flints in the eighteenth and nineteenth century, as this developed into one of Britain's biggest industries and for a while we supplied the world with quality gun flints in their millions.

Brandon in Norfolk was the centre of the industry and firstly 'floor stone' was mined to obtain the very best quality. The nodules were quartered and large blades removed, all the work being done with metal hammers and metal anvils. Each blade narrowed from proximal to distal end and this allowed gun

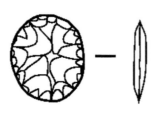

Produce a thin circular disc and sharpen 360 degrees around.

A discoidal knife (production and finished item).

flints of various sizes to be removed so each blade could make four or five gun flints. These were used in muskets, carbines and pistols. By 1900, to give an idea of the industry, a man earned 3 shillings and six pence for a ten-hour day and 1,000 musket flints were priced at 5 shillings. The work was hard and because the knapping was done indoors silicosis took its toll and not many workers lived beyond their 30s.

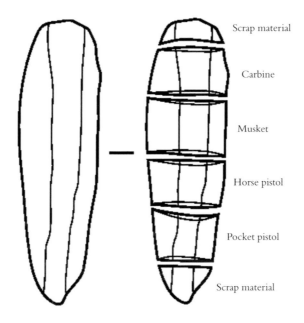

Scrap material

Carbine

Musket

Horse pistol

Pocket pistol

Scrap material

A double-ridged flake was struck, which was then divided as shown.

Gun flint knapping.

The work was repetitious but the exponents were masters of the craft, especially the taking of blades from the core. Each core, if struck properly and continuously, can produce over 100 blades that were then severed up into individual gun flints. The reduction of the blades was done on a metal anvil, which was a bevelled metal bar. The blade was placed upon the sharpened edge of the anvil and struck with a small hammer that made a squared edge severing a finished gun flint. The technique can be tried using a brick bolster mounted upside down in a wooden black. It is not that difficult a process to learn and experimentation will soon show the angle the blade needs to be held at and the point of striking.

7

METAL AND
MODERN TOOLS

Up to now we have concentrated on the original tools of the Stone Age, hammer stones and antlers etc., but modern knapping techniques have produced a range of other materials that can effectively be used. If you wish to stay with the authentic tools of the period and be a purist, then by all means do so, but even for a trial period do have a go with modern knapping techniques.

The hard hammer can be replaced by copper rod or a made up copper 'bopper' to use its American description. Aluminium is not usually heavy enough and brass, phosphor bronze and steel do not work. Copper is best as it's soft enough to 'grip' the flint. A length of solid copper rod works well or you can purchase a copper pipe end cap and make a bopper. If you are using solid rod, a selection of sizes is required. To provide grip, wrap sticky tape around the centre section. Sizes can be from 75mm up to 5cm or 6cm, although the thicker copper rod can be expensive. The end of the rod needs to be rounded to start but with use, you naturally tend to develop a spherical end. Your local scrapyard should be able to provide all you need as you can usually purchase by weight and a bar will last a lifetime.

If you are making a bopper, any DIY store that sells plumbing requirements will have copper end caps again in a variety of sizes. You will need wooden dowel the same size as the end cap bore. With a blowlamp melt some lead (again a tiny amount from your scrapyard) into the end cap for added weight and then glue the cap to the end of the dowel. If you want the bopper to be a bit heavier, solder in a few centimetres of copper pipe and follow the same process, only this time the dowel needs to be a bit smaller to fit into the short piece of pipe.

Many of the boppers are modified by doming the end with a punch to create a spherical shape or by hammering the end cap on to a rounded-off bar.

Modern percussors, made from solid copper, or a domed copper cap filled with lead to provide weight. Shown here are wooden-handled copper and lead boppers, a solid copper rod, and solid copper ends set into an aluminium tube with a wooden core. A range of boppers is required: the heavier, robust type for big jobs and the smaller, lighter type for delicate work.

For making a 'pressure flaker' you can use a copper rod 50mm to 75mm diameter mounted into a wooden file handle, or your Ships Chandler will supply a range of copper nails from 8in and less (for some strange reason nails still seem to be sold in imperial sizes). Whatever you use, the tip should be filed to a point like a pencil. As copper hardens when it is struck, beating a point on an anvil with a hammer and then finishing with a file is a better way to make the pressure flaker point.

Quite often pressure flakers can be quite long and used under your arm for greater force; these are called ishi sticks after their inventor, a North American Indian. The tip is exactly the same as a hand pressure flaker only the shaft supporting the tip is longer.

One thing about copper is that the more you work it, or hammer it, the harder it becomes and conversely if you anneal it, that is heat to cherry red and dip in cold water, it will become softer. So the basic shape of the end of the rod needs to be hammered into shape rather than filed.

Small pressure flakers are required for making the slot in the base of an arrowhead and smaller copper nails are very good, as they are quite hard copper. Rather than a pointed end a flaker that is shaped like a screwdriver, and used edge-on can be quite a valuable tool.

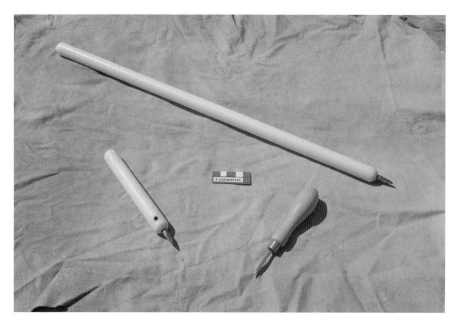

Three pressure flakers with the very long ishi stick. The smaller hand pressure flaker and a very fine, tiny detail flaker. The white flakers have an Allen key screw fitting to allow blades to be changed and the tiny flaker is a hardened steel flaker with a boxwood handle.

Over the last few years a number of pressure flaking machines or jigs have been made and these will be discussed later on when we deal with pressure flaking slabs. Diamond wheel tile cutters, which you can find in any DIY or tool centre, can be very useful especially for the preparing of blanks for glass. A trip to your local glass merchant will show that usually they have a stack of odd ends of glass of various thicknesses and for a small fee they will cut you up strips of 4cm or 5cm wide. For a few pounds you can obtain sufficient glass to last several months of knapping. The strips can be used to make long pressure flaked blades or, by using your tile cutter, you can make arrowhead blanks.

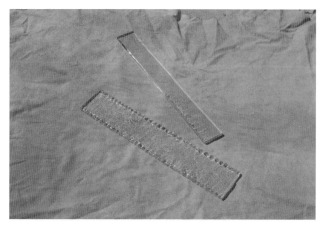

5mm glass blanks cut from a sheet using a tile-cutting machine with a diamond blade. These are glass arrowhead blanks ready for pressure flaking.

If you are using glass you will find that a glass cutter leaves a smooth edge that your pressure flaker will slip on, so the edges need to be ground and the best tool for this is a grind wheel. Make sure that it is a grind wheel and not one of those impregnated discs that are sold for use in a hand grinder for stone slab or metal cutting. The grind wheel needs to be a rough grit variety and is a once-only purchase, as it will last a lifetime. Your local tool shop should also sell smaller type grind wheels for use in a hand drill and these are quite cheap and readily useable for many tasks in the knapping process.

A whole series of mini grind wheels and broken larger grind wheels used as abraders. Any rough stone can be used but grind wheels work well and are very cheap. Millstone grit works well if it can be obtained, as well as hard sandstone.

Modern materials can also provide a cheap alternative to leather for pressure flaking pads and for knee pads. The cost of a piece of leather of sufficient thickness, at least 50mm, to go over your knee can be quite high, as you will find out if you visit your local saddle maker. The alternative is a piece of carpet as we have already mentioned, or rubber ribbed car mat suitably cut to size works just as well to support thinner leather. Literally any thick material that will protect your knee will suffice.

For pressure flaking the use of a pad for the hand is desirable, as the carry through of the tool can inflict a deep gouge in your unprotected hand. Many knappers use a simple piece of fairly thick leather wrapped around the workpiece, but this has one disadvantage. When the pressure wave is travelling through your piece of flint anything touching the surface in the wave's path can result in the termination of the flake. Ideally, the area to be knapped should be free of contact, so solid hand pads have been developed. These pads can be made from any suitable material and it has been found that old conveyer belt works beautifully, but that may be difficult to find. The strength of this material is that it is made from rubber bonded to canvas. A really good alternative is a lorry mud guard, so a quick visit to a breakers yard with your Stanley knife works or a purchase from a lorry parts supplier will again give you a one-off purchase, as just one mud guard will last a lifetime.

The pad should have two layers, a bottom slice to stop the pressure flaker digging in and a top slice with a slot cut into it so the flint can be held against this top slice with the path of the flint over the slot, so at no point of the pressure wave travel is anything touching the flint.

Virtually any tough material can be used as a pressure pad, as its function is to protect the hand from the pressure flaker on any carry-through of stroke or tool slip. A three-slice glued leather pad is shown, as well as the author's preference for an aluminium, copper circuit board and truck mud flap sandwich. There are layers of mud flap glued together with circuit board between them to prevent skidding on the harder aluminium.

The size of the flake pad is dependent on the size of your hand, as it must fit comfortably and allow your hand to wrap around and hold the flint. For a small hand, 8cm by 4cm is about right but trial and error needs to be the order of the day. Care also should be taken not to make the pad too thick, but once the size is ascertained, the slices should be glued together. The pad in the picture above is made from a piece of aluminium glued to a piece of copper circuit board for non-slippage, as the tool will dig into the copper and the top slot surface lorry mud guard. The angle of the slot is determined by the fact that the pressure flaker is pushed in a line towards the second joint of the index finger, when in use, so this again is a matter of handedness.

As your knapping progresses you build up your own toolkit and can add things like a high tensile steel bradawl for tiny finishing flakes. This use of modern tools is entirely up to you. Many people like to be purists and remain solely with the original tools of the Stone Age. There is no right or wrong way with this as it comes down to your preference and how you wish to enjoy your knapping. There is, however, no alternative to learning the use of the original tools and no shortcut to perfecting a mastery of knapping; you have to persevere for many hours to achieve the required standard.

The technique of knapping is one of the things in life that looks so easy when you watch an expert but can be frustrating when you try and copy. The saving grace is the sense of achievement when you do succeed.

8

PRESSURE FLAKING

Having looked at the tools for pressure flaking, there is one rule that we must have that is obvious – you must have a platform to initiate the flake, otherwise the flaker just slips off the flint.

The pressure flaker must have somewhere to grip, as the act of flaking is that pressure is built up against the flint until the critical point is reached and the material being flaked gives way. If you are trying to pressure off a flake that is too big, then all that happens is you find you are not strong enough to complete the task. The obvious solution is not to try and do too much or swap the hand technique for a leg technique that gives a greater force, as leg muscles are more powerful than arm muscles.

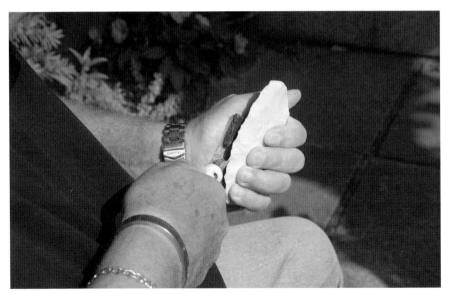

An over-the-shoulder view of hand pressure flaking; remember the hand remains still and the path of pressure is towards the knuckle of the index finger. If you alter this line then the flakes will be shorter.

The pressure pad is parallel to the ground and the action of closing the legs will produce a pressure line towards the index finger knuckle. This position is not easy to replicate and beginners usually find they cannot use their leg strength as it becomes counter-intuitive to use the force of closing your legs when the action still seems orientated about the hands and shoulders.

Your flaking tool should be sharpened like a pencil if it's copper or brought to a wedge-shaped point if it's an antler tine, and as soon as your tip blunts then it should be re-sharpened. Place the tip of the tool a little way into the platform and increase the pressure in a backward motion towards the back of your hand at the knuckle of your index finger. Increase the pressure until the tool clicks. It is a very distinctive sound and when this happens, the tool will have removed a flake from the flint. The edge of the flake scar will now be a guide for the next flake, so move about 40mm to 50mm along the platform and take a second flake if needed from the platform. Repeat the process by preparing the platform by abrading and then flaking. Each ridge you create will be a guide for following flakes. If you are working on a slab or the continuous edge of a worked blade, then by abrading you will have a continuous platform that you can work along.

If you are starting a slab the first flake will be rounded, but subsequent flakes will be elongated as they find a scar to follow. If your flakes are not going very far into the flint, then the error is either insufficient force or more likely the angle of attack of the flaking tool.

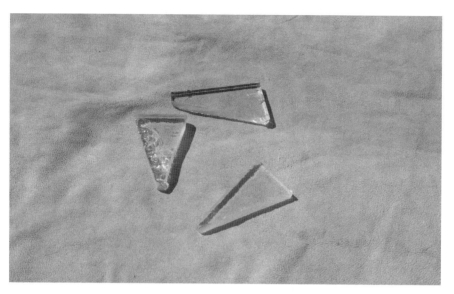

5mm glass blanks cut from a sheet using a tile-cutting machine with a diamond blade. These are glass arrowhead blanks ready for pressure flaking. Two pieces of 5mm 'window' glass part flaked to show the process of making a glass point. The edges of the glass are abraded after being cut from a sheet with a glass cutter and then pressure flaked using an ishi stick on the bigger slab and a hand flaker on the smaller. The next stage would be a second pass to create a sharp edge and then a reduction of the end to produce a point.

If the technique is not clear at this point, then go on to the Internet and look at 'flint knapping' in your search engine. You will find lots of demonstrations of knapping techniques especially from the channel 'Palaeomanjim' on YouTube. This is Jim Winn, a fellow knapper, who has made many 'how to knap' videos and produces some truly wonderful work. Jim mainly works in obsidian, volcanic glass, which is easier to work than flint.

A good idea is to obtain a glass slab about 5cm wide and 50mm thick and about 12cm long. Abrade all the edges so they are fully opaque and there are no shiny spots left. Hold the glass in the pad and put the pressure flaker a few millimetres in from both the end and the lower side.

Take off your first flake and then work the whole length as shown, taking flakes every few millimetres working down the edge from left to right. Try and get the flakes to reach the centre of the slab on each flaking. When you have flaked the whole edge, turn it around and repeat the process, this time getting your flakes to reach across and meet up with the flakes from the first pass. Sometimes the flakes do not meet if your technique is not consistent. If this happens do not try and correct the position at this time. When you have flaked the whole side turn the slab over and do the same on the other side.

A word of warning here, if you are getting tired then take a break, as if you start to overdo the effort you will make more mistakes and achieve shorter length to your flakes. If you have completed the task correctly your slab should now look like the diagrams opposite.

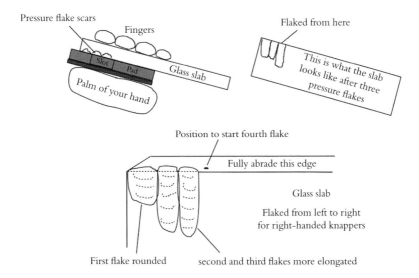

Pressure flake scars

Fingers

Flaked from here

Slot Pad

Glass slab

Palm of your hand

This is what the slab looks like after three pressure flakes

Position to start fourth flake

Fully abrade this edge

Glass slab

Flaked from left to right
for right-handed knappers

First flake rounded

second and third flakes more elongated

Pressure flaking (1).

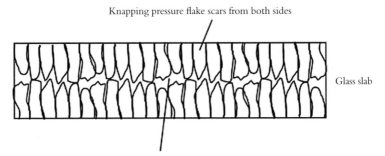

Knapping pressure flake scars from both sides

Glass slab

You may have areas after the first pass
that the knapping has not reached

Pressure flaking (2).

The slab should now be abraded along both sides. This will create a series of platforms for another pass over the whole length of both sides. You can start at one end and make new flakes, this time using the position on the edge where you get a peak between two previous flakes. If you are doing the technique correctly, the second pass should travel further into the slab and remove all the un-flaked areas from the surface.

Please remember that glass in its manufacturing process contains inherent strains in its fabric and sometimes you can feel the differences, as areas of the glass will be harder than others. Also occasionally you can hit an unseen strain that will fracture the glass. This can happen and it is not your fault but you end up with two short slabs instead of the one you started with.

The making of second and subsequent passes should be for thinning the piece, so it is very important to ensure that you are driving flakes right across or at least three quarters of the way across the slab, otherwise the sides become thin and the centre still stays quite thick. The narrowing of the ends to make a tip and a back require you to continue to make platforms and drive flakes across the centre line, so do not allow the thinning process to stop just because you are trying to alter the shape of the slab.

Three finished glass points. Two arrow/spear points notched and an elongated flaked blade.

The final part of your pressure flaking of a slab requires the sides to be evened up and sharpened and slots to be made in the tail. The procedure for 'slotting' requires either a small pointed copper nail or a screwdriver shape that is thin in one direction. Try practising on any old flake by holding the flaker at 90 degrees to the flake that is flat on your pad. Very near the edge of the flake, press vertically down and you will remove a tiny flake. Turn the piece over and you will see a tiny scar where the cone of fracture happened. Using this scar, press down again and remove a new flake. Continue doing this, turning the workpiece over each time. Slowly work your way into the flake and you will produce a slot the size of your flaker. With a chisel point keep the flat heading into the slot.

A word of caution when doing this – the flaker must be at 90 degrees because if it's slightly out of true, you will cause a sideways break in the flake and remove a big chunk. When you are proficient at this, try slotting the end of your flaked slab. The sides of the point can be regularised by abrading and then finally the sharp edge added with very small close flaking.

Working from a slab is much easier than reducing a flake or a core down and then proceeding with pressure flaking, but once you have become accomplished at thinning and pressure flaking, the whole process can be undertaken.

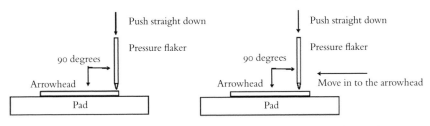

Hold the arrowhead against the pad, ensuring there is good contact at the flaking point, press down vertically and push off a small flake.

Important note

You must always have the pressure flaker vertical in all axis, otherwise you exert sideways pressure and will break the ears off of the arrowhead.

Reverse the arrowhead and repeat the process, this time using the flake scar as the platform for the second removal.

Keep reversing the arrowhead and removing flakes until the slot is long enough.

Take the flakes in very small increments and do not try to rush the process.

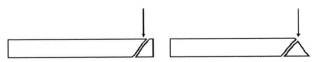

The first flake leaves a scar as shown.

Using the scar as a platform, take the second flake, keep reversing and take further flakes.

Diagram of slotting.

9

ANOTHER VIEWPOINT ON STARTING TO FLINT KNAP

We have come a long way in our knapping so at this point it may be worthwhile to recap by looking at some comments from a different person's 'take' on the art of knapping. Mark Ford is a fellow knapper who has, over several years, become quite accomplished at the production of stone tools.

He has been asked to produce some notes as to what he has learnt and the mistakes and corrections he made while attempting to perfect the art.

Mark writes:

Holding an 'original' stone tool made many thousands of years ago is amazing enough, but to be able to look at it, smugly grin, and say 'ah, yes, I had that trouble only yesterday!' sums up what I find fascinating with the practice of flint knapping. Simply put, it opens up a connection that spans the millennia. We don't have any writing, language or stories from most of our pre-history, yet a simple stone tool actually contains an intimate record of the maker's thought process waiting to be 'read' by those who understand the art of knapping. The world may have changed but many things remain exactly the same, like hinge fractures, frost flaws, and those annoying fossil inclusions! These all plagued prehistoric people just as they do to us today.

When I first began knapping, I started off as many people do, by doing a one-day knapping course. After the obligatory health and safety talk, disclaimer form completion, selection of goggles, gloves, knee pads etc. we started off by making stinging nettle string. This is made by stripping the outer skin from wilted stinging nettle stalks. The outer skin is carefully peeled off in long strips and hung up to dry. When dry, the nettle strips are twisted together, in groups of three to make an excellent cord, which is surprisingly strong. Next, we made a simple scraper, by striking a previously struck flint piece (using a small pebble) in just one direction, only hitting on the curved side of the flint so that a half moon-shaped 'cut out' was made on the edge. By striking in just one direction, the scraper gets the perfect single-sided bevel edge that's needed to work wood, in this case ideal for removing the bark on a hazel stick!

Next we took a struck knife blade blank, shaped it by using both a small hammer stone and an antler point, also a saw was made by notching a flint flake. We used the saw to make a hafted knife handle. Let me tell you, sawing a hazel stick using a flint saw tool is something you only try once! It took at least half an hour to saw through the knife handle, but all of these stages taught me just how much effort must have gone into making what we today regard as a simple tool. The flint blade was then set into a slit in the hazel handle and bound with the nettle string before being sealed with beeswax and pine resin glue. This fairly simple series of steps actually covered all of the basic steps needed to start off knapping. I would certainly recommend making a basic flint knife and scraper as a first step, as the frustration of not achieving anything is what puts most people off persevering any further.

It was many months after doing my knapping course that I began attempting what I later learned was called a 'biface'. (Sooner or later the appeal of making a massive axe becomes irresistible.) I started by striking a chunk of beach flint with another equally sized chunk of beach flint, which of course shattered (as hammer stones should ideally be nice and round so that the shock wave doesn't cause it to break – lesson learned!).

The second thing I learned was thin edges flake far easier than thick ones. Trying to remove too much material in one go is a common mistake, as you can end up with a large, ugly deep flake usually from the opposite end of where you expected! People will tell you the theory and the technical jargon, but if you remember only one golden rule you will not go far wrong – it's that the flint 'platform' you are hitting must have an angle of less than 90 degrees underneath it, otherwise it will either shatter or fracture internally. Imagine hitting a house brick with its 90 degree angled sides – it would just shatter wouldn't it? Once you have been knapping for a while, this really will become automatic, but when you are starting out it will probably seem near impossible to get. I can only say stick with it, and you will find it suddenly clicks.

There are times when this <90-degree angle rule has to be relaxed a little, such as when first breaking into a large rounded nodule of flint; you sometimes have to just bite the bullet and whack it, though you must always strike a flint nodule where it is most likely to break (isolated protruding nodules, thinner areas and natural flat areas are all good striking places to start you off).

Once you have a freshly broken platform you can then begin the process of removing flakes. I found I had real trouble at first, when chopping up large chunks of flint into smaller manageable chunks (a process called quartering). It seemed to me that I wasn't hitting hard enough to break the flint but after several more goes it suddenly became clear that I was in fact just hitting the flint in the wrong place! When I hit it in a weaker place I found it required hardly any effort at all. Careful thought about where you are hitting is every bit as important as how hard you hit.

Making a simple hand axe can take you three minutes or three hours, depending on how much refinement you want to achieve and what material you have to work with. Where I live, I have access to beach flint, which occurs in fairly rounded nodules, so once I have removed a lucky first flake from the nodule, I will be aiming to remove the outer cortex of the flint as a first step. Cortex (the white outer coating on a flint nodule) is horrid to knap. It absorbs the shock wave and causes all sorts of issues.

You obviously have to start with the flake you first made if you are working on a fully cortex covered pebble. By turning over the flint and removing a flake right next to the previous one you just removed and alternating like this from side to side each time, you can work right around the flint until you have something that is fairly flat and roughly symmetrical in profile, with the classic zigzag shape when viewed from the side and little or no cortex. Remember that a flake will always follow a ridge in the flint, so the previous flake scar is what you rely on to carry the next flake along the flint.

You should remove as much cortex as possible, but sometimes there are a few areas that will prove too difficult. Provided the cortex doesn't interfere with the final stages of the hand axe, it can be left on. Hand axes are narrower at one end, so pay attention to the shape. By removing more material from the pointed end, it can be shaped as desired. Now you need to work around the edges, removing smaller and smaller flakes from both sides until the edges are nice and straight. When it looks tidy, it's finished. The golden rule is if you think it's finished it probably is time to stop! Many a time knappers have taken off just one more fatal flake, only to find the piece breaks or something unexpected ruins it. Most of the time prehistoric people were making a functional tool. I suspect they were not unduly bothered with making it look pretty, more likely their work looked pretty due to the endless practice they would have had.

Proper selection of flint is an important subject for the newcomer to understand. Normally the more a piece of flint rings when tapped the better quality it will be. I have however found, particularly with beach flint, that it's the size of the pebble that actually determines how well it will or will not ring (due to resonance), so it's often not until you have removed cortex that you will see exactly how good the flint is. A good rule of thumb is to go for uniform clean looking flint with no obvious cracks and of a suitable size (bearing in mind removing cortex will considerably reduce the size). If your selected piece of flint rings like a bell then even better! Costal flint is obviously subject to the sea, so it gets smashed around quite a bit. It is, however, possible to find very good quality flint on our shores where the local rock type is chalk or limestone. Some of the best flint I have ever knapped has come from a beach.

Inland flint bearing areas such as Norfolk are where the truly good flint occurs, especially from underground seams. Surface flint is normally either damaged by ploughing or frost fractured, however, some good flint can be found on the surface, especially at the edges of ploughed fields. Flint has been mined in Norfolk for thousands of years, as mined flint has far superior knapping qualities since it has not been exposed to the weather. I would recommend trying Norfolk flint if you can get hold of it.

One technique that a newcomer will soon want to master is pressure flaking. The process involves removing small flakes by using a pointed tool, usually an antler or a copper point. Experimentation has shown that copper is by far the best material to pressure flake with, as it is just the right hardness to produce good flakes. Antler usually works well too, however, with gener-ally smaller flakes and the need to reshape the edge. I would also recommend getting some good leather gloves, as shards of flint (or glass) are especially sharp, and make yourself a pad of thick rubber (ideally sandwiched with a sheet of thin aluminium to stop sharp points going into your hand). Good pressure flaking is all about preparation of the workpiece. Abrading the edge to be flaked is very important to stop the point slipping. I found early on that a piece of broken grinding wheel stone was ideal to roughen the edge. Careful control of your arms to allow steady, precise pressure and practice is the key to good pressure flaking. The flaker point should be fairly sharp and when pressing into the material, a little lift at the last minute can help to start the flake off. It is vital to start your next flake next to the last one, as the flake will follow the ridge left by the previous flake scar.

I use pieces of 3mm glass as practice pieces (off-cuts from a local glass merchant are ideal), though avoid toughened glass as it won't work! Don't be afraid to experiment. It is quite surprising what materials will knap – glass, obsidian, flint, beer bottles and even old kitchen ceramic sinks.

Above all enjoy it, as the beauty of this hobby is you never stop learning, especially when you meet up with other knappers and can show your latest piece of handiwork.

10

A Further Look at How you Hit Rocks: The Levallois Reduction

round 200,000 years ago the Acheulian hand axe makers, the Neanderthals, produced a technique that manufactured a bifacial flake tool or an arrowpoint, ready for use, by preparing a core before striking off the desired item. This has been called the 'Levallois' technique. The struck flakes were used with very little retouch as they were removed with a completely sharp edge and therefore were ready for use. Levallois tools are very wasteful in the amount of material discarded and each core will only produce a small number of desired flakes. Production is usually found only in areas of abundant flint nodules.

Stage 1
Select a rounded nodule and remove flakes 360 degrees.

Stage 2
Flake using the previous flake scars and turn into a dome or turtle-back shape.

Stage 3
Prepare a platform for the removal of the Levallois flake.

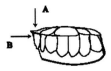

The Levallois flake.

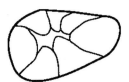

Stage 4
Abrade and strengthen the platform A. Strike off the Levallois flake B.

The remaining cone.

The dorsal side of the Levallois flake will have radial flaking, while the ventral side will have the bulb of percussion.

Another look at the Levallois reduction to make a biface.

The bifacial tool was produced by preparing the core with a domed top and is often referred to as a 'turtle back' because of its shape. A cobble was flaked around its periphery for the full 360 degrees, usually from one side, and the flake scars were then used as platforms to remove the top of the cobble in a circular pattern, reversing the core before striking.

The profile of the dome or turtle back could be controlled by the angle of flake removal; an abrupt angle of strike produced a heavily domed core and an oblique strike produced a more flattened core. One end of the dome was then prepared and heavily abraded to produce a very strong platform and then the finished flake was struck. The removed flake was now biconvex as the dome was the dorsal side and the bulb of percussion produced a convex face on the ventral side.

If the flake was used as a hand axe, then the dome was steeply angled and the bulb quite large for a considerable strength blow, but if used as an arrowhead blank, the dome was more shallow and the bulb smaller by soft hammer or more careful removal. The core preparation was therefore carefully thought out and dependent on the requirements of the knapper and the flake's final usage.

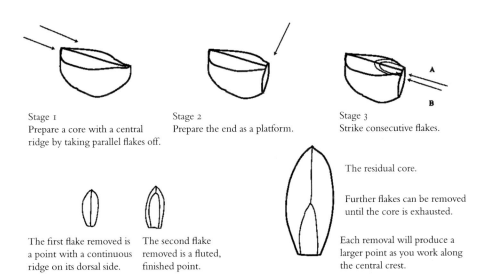

Stage 1
Prepare a core with a central ridge by taking parallel flakes off.

Stage 2
Prepare the end as a platform.

Stage 3
Strike consecutive flakes.

The first flake removed is a point with a continuous ridge on its dorsal side.

The second flake removed is a fluted, finished point.

The residual core.

Further flakes can be removed until the core is exhausted.

Each removal will produce a larger point as you work along the central crest.

Levallois point, subsequent point and final product.

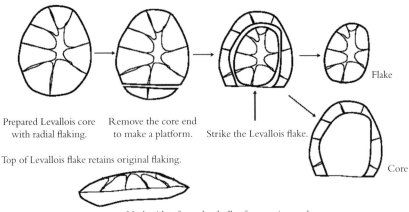

Prepared Levallois core　　Remove the core end
with radial flaking.　　　to make a platform.　　Strike the Levallois flake.

Flake

Top of Levallois flake retains original flaking.

Core

Underside of core has bulb of percussion and
flake ripples from being struck.
The bulb can now be removed if required.

Further detail on the Levallois flake removal.

The core did not have to be circular, as an elongated sausage-shaped core would allow long blade removal. In central France, in the Le Grande Presigne area, where the raw material is a honey-coloured chert, Neanderthals produced long blades up to 35cm long from an elongated Levallois core, named *livre de beurre* (a pound of butter).

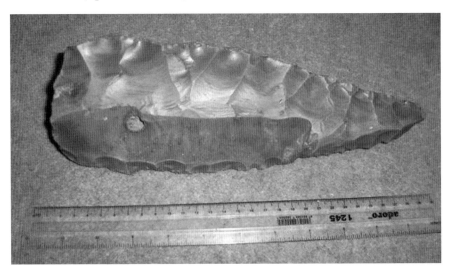

Made from Le Grande Presigne this is a livre de beurre *or elongated Levallois core used for the manufacture of long blades. The core was radial-flaked at each end and flaked in from both sides to make an elongated hump. The end was then struck to create a platform and the flake removed. Several flakes can be removed from this type of core, but in this instance the removal of the first flake revealed a fossil within the core that made further removals impossible. The core was then discarded.*

If the core was to produce a finished arrowhead then a different preparation was required. From the scars of the peripheral flaking, two platforms were prepared and parallel rejuvenation flakes were struck to make a crest on the core.

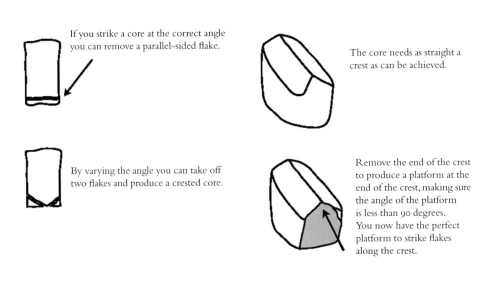

If you strike a core at the correct angle you can remove a parallel-sided flake.

The core needs as straight a crest as can be achieved.

By varying the angle you can take off two flakes and produce a crested core.

Remove the end of the crest to produce a platform at the end of the crest, making sure the angle of the platform is less than 90 degrees. You now have the perfect platform to strike flakes along the crest.

The Levallois crested core.

The end of the crest was prepared as a platform so a flake could be struck that was equidistant each side of the crest and ran about a third of its length. This first flake was discarded and a platform was prepared to take a second flake from the same position. The second flake was then struck larger than the first flake in both width and length to produce a completed arrowhead already fluted for mounting in a shaft. Because this was a flake that was feathered out on the core, it was sufficiently sharp and ready for use.

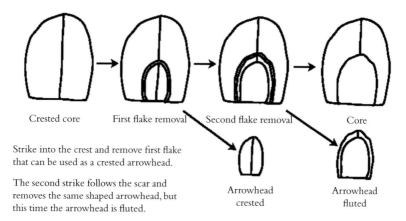

Crested core   First flake removal   Second flake removal   Core

Strike into the crest and remove first flake that can be used as a crested arrowhead.

The second strike follows the scar and removes the same shaped arrowhead, but this time the arrowhead is fluted.

Further removals of fluted arrowheads may be accomplished until the crest is utilised, but arrowheads get larger with each removal.

Arrowhead crested

Arrowhead fluted

The Levallois arrowhead.

Further flakes could now be removed until the full width of the core was reached. At this point the core could be rejuvenated and a new crest established that allowed the whole process to be repeated.

11

A Core Tool and a Blade Tool

We must now consider the requirements for reduction of large nodules and odd-shaped rocks to allow the manufacture of flint tools. We looked earlier at the two different types of tools, the core tool where you reduce down a nodule to make a finished tool, and the making of a blade core so blade production can take place. These two processes require different strategies. Firstly, make it easy on yourself. If there is a large choice of raw material, select the items nearest to your requirements rather than making working difficulties that can be avoided. Often, though, the availability of raw material is restricted so we must make the best of what we have.

The very worst case is the spherical solid nodule as it is hard to break open, which is why hammer stones are so strong. Nature usually does not make the perfect sphere, so nodules will come in all shapes and sizes. The initial thought process is to have some idea of what you are trying to achieve. You have to imagine the finished tool trapped within the nodule and all you are doing is releasing it. This is not such a silly idea, as you are laying down a strategy for how to tackle an amorphous lump of flint to produce your own work of art.

Quite often the nodule will be elongated and have protrusions that can be easily removed. Always take the path of least resistance and think that the narrowest part of the nodule will break the easiest. After removing the odd protrusions look for natural platforms, especially the end of an elongated nodule, as when the first break is made, it will automatically become the platform for further fractures and allow you to get further into the centre.

Remember that cortex does not carry a shock wave easily so you need to expose the inside of the nodule to get a good platform for 'quartering' your nodule. The term means splitting up a nodule and not dividing it into four.

If you have a fairly round nodule, then to split it in two you need to have a glancing blow, about 20 or 30 degrees off vertical, as the shatter cone needs to be offset to allow the fracture. Once the nodule is in half then it can be dealt with, as shown later on in this chapter.

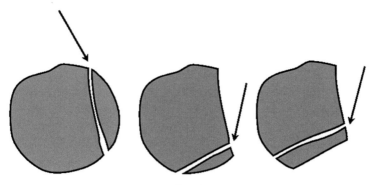

Remove a flake from the nodule.

Using the flake scar as a platform, strike at an angle to remove a primary spall.

Using the same angle, strike a second spall. If the angle is the same as before, the resultant spall will have parallel sides.

Quartering a spherical nodule.

If the nodule is more 'flying saucer'-shaped, then a different strategy can be adopted dependent on the angle of strike and the force used allowing you to achieve your required result. The set-up angle will give a range of flake lengths and the position of the strike will determine the thickness of the flake.

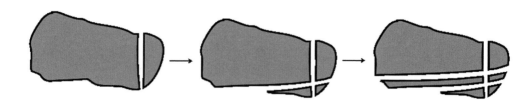

Whatever the shape of the nodule, the same principle applies as with the spherical nodule. Create a platform and take a spall, or series of spalls, using the same angle of attack.

Quartering an elongated nodule.

One of the main objectives is to remove as much of the cortex as possible and although total removal is not a necessity, it is always more aesthetically pleasing to produce a finished item free of cortex.

The strategy for a core reduction tool is usually the elongated hand axe shape, so the longest length of the nodule is normally selected as the major axis of the finished tool. Bear in mind that in many cases you are trying to get a parallel-sided biconvex shape, so plan for this from the first strike. You may have to work completely around your nodule-removing cortex before you can start the shaping or thinning process. Take a small flake off at an appropriate place and then reverse the nodule and you will find that the flake removed provides an excellent platform for the next removal. Keep rotating the nodule on each strike and eventually you will have progressed all the way round and have produced a zigzag profile that is ideal for further reductions.

Many beginners make the mistake of not planning the thinning strategy early enough in the process and get one side of the profile flat but the other side with a peak, so the cross section of the workpiece is roughly triangular. The tendency is then to try and remove the 'peak' by taking further flakes from the flat side, which only makes the matter worse and also reduces the width of the flint.

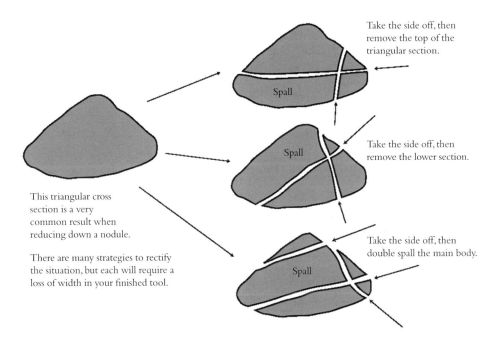

Take the side off, then remove the top of the triangular section.

Spall

Take the side off, then remove the lower section.

Spall

This triangular cross section is a very common result when reducing down a nodule.

There are many strategies to rectify the situation, but each will require a loss of width in your finished tool.

Take the side off, then double spall the main body.

Spall

Correcting a triangular shape cross section.

Although you lose width, the only salvation in this case is to work from the 'peak' side. This seems counterproductive at first, as you are changing the axis line of your tool, but eventually you will regain the desired thickness width ratio.

The biggest problem the beginner faces is trying to reduce a misshapen nodule into the desired shape of a parallel-sided flat rough-out. Although only experience will help, some tips are helpful. Look at your nodule as much as you can and try to see the shape you require. Always go for mass first to try and reduce the unwanted material. Often people will find a perfect ridge and try and remove the next flake without considering the result. You cannot remove a mass unless there is a platform to strike from and many times you have to sacrifice length or width to create the platform. Many publications on knapping show the thinning process but it is always from an already shaped workpiece. You will not usually be in that position.

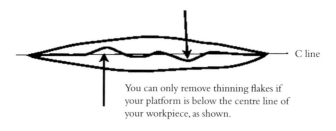

C line

You can only remove thinning flakes if your platform is below the centre line of your workpiece, as shown.

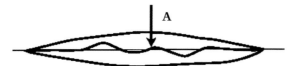

A

If you want to remove a flake from position A then you must lower the centre line, as shown below.

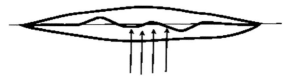

Take a series of small nibbles to lower the centre line.

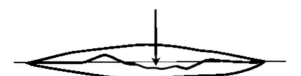

Once the platform is below the centre line the thinning flake can be removed.

Note
The nibbles may be counter-intuitive as you lower the platform towards the strike of the nibbles. Many people get this wrong and move the platform in the opposite direction by hitting from the wrong side. View the diagram carefully.

Selecting the centre line and lowering the platform.

The only real help that I can give is to analyse the shape in cross section terms. Recognise the mass you want to get rid of and see if there is a platform available to carry out the task. If the platform does not exist, work out how to produce the platform, as in the diagram showing how to correct a triangular (see page 87) cross section.

Now seems an appropriate time to introduce the concept of thinning a biface. This is by always taking a flake off when the platform is below the centre line of the tool being thinned. Again it seems counter-intuitive but to lower the platform below the centre line requires that you nibble away the edge of the current platform on what appears to be the wrong side.

When you have your rough-out completed and are ready to start thinning, hold up the flint so that the profile is facing you and imagine the centre line of the profile. To start with you can take a felt-tip pen and draw the centre line on the flint. Only the parts of the edge below or above the centre line are potential platforms, as there is no use trying to take a flake off where the strike line crosses the centre line. Also remember that the edges are sharp and to make them into potential platforms you must abrade to strengthen the platform. Do this every time before any flake removal, otherwise all that will happen is that you crush the platform and develop a series of hinge fractures on the edge of your workpiece. Removing these hinges is very difficult when you are trying to take off thin further removal flakes. In fact, it can eventually be impossible and ruin your workpiece.

To return to quartering, let us look at the half nodule. The flat surface is now suitable for making a blade core or producing a spall for core reduction tools, or a mixture of both. The flat surface is a perfect platform for your next stage and only requires you to decide what you wish to produce.

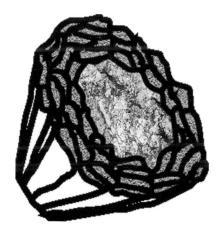

Working a divided nodule for blades.

Strike the flat surface of the nodule near the edge with sufficient force and you will separate off a flake that should feather out near the bottom of the nodule. Insufficient force and the flake will terminate part way down in a hinge fracture. Work round the nodule removing flakes (now called blades) and you will eventually produce a Mousterian or prismatic core blank. To remove further blades you will need to abrade the top edge, as the preceding blade will leave a tiny lip that must be removed before further working. This core can be used to make dozens of blades over and over again until it becomes too small to work.

A word of warning here, if you hit with insufficient force or miss your platform and produce a hinge fracture, you cannot take a further blade to remove the hinge by hitting again in the same place. If you try this you will make the hinge worse, as subsequent blades will terminate at the same spot. A remedy is to reverse the core and take a blade from the other end, making a bipolar core. An outside chance to recover the situation is to replace the flake in its scar and hit it a second time, but often this will not work.

The angle of strike on the flat surface is crucial, as again you are using the cone of shatter to run parallel to the side of the core, so an angle of between 45 and 50 degrees is ideal.

To use the half nodule for a parallel-sided core tool you will need to use a different strategy.

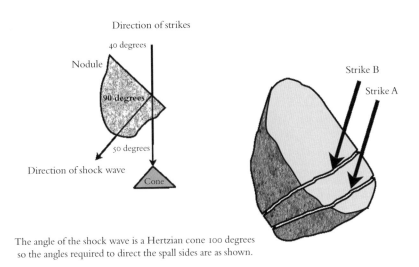

The angle of the shock wave is a Hertzian cone 100 degrees so the angles required to direct the spall sides are as shown.

Working a divided nodule for spalls.

To reduce down a half nodule for a spall for a hand axe or an elongated biface the strike must be at an oblique angle and well into the nodule. This strike requires considerable force and you must divide the half core, as shown in the diagram opposite, in two separate places. This leaves you with a parallel-sided spall that is ready for further work.

The strategy for each nodule will be different and it is impossible to give instructions for every occasion. You just have to gain experience in knowing what to hit, where to hit, how to hit and how much force is needed. Suffice it to say that quartering is one of the difficult areas of knapping but your perseverance will eventually produce results.

One of the things to remember is that flakes always follow ridges, so by creating a platform at the base of a ridge you will invariably get your flake to follow the ridge 'path'. This means that you will have some idea of predicting where your fracture line will travel.

We have looked at various core and blade tools and their reduction from a large nodule and you will now realise that there is a certain amount of overlap, so determining the method of production is a matter of choice and of taking the easiest path to your desired goal.

Removing and using a large blade will give sufficient material to work completely both the dorsal and ventral sides, but the blade must be flat to produce the same result as reducing a core. Quite often the removal of a large blade will give a curved profile but if working a blade is your desired method, then the blade core must be prepared with parallel sides so a flat blade can be removed.

The more you work flint the more you learn its eccentricities and how to achieve your aims.

12

LET'S MAKE A THIN BIFACE

The aim of every knapper is how to reduce a nodule by percussion to obtain a thin biface, the end result being measured in the ratio of thickness to width. With skill it is possible to get beyond the magic 8 to 1 ratio and even achieve 10 or 12 to 1.

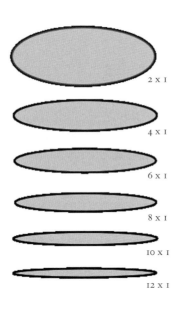

2 x 1

4 x 1

In lithic reproduction the cross section of the tool is measured by comparing the width of the piece to its thickness.

6 x 1

8 x 1

10 x 1

12 x 1

Thickness/width ratio for the cross section of a biface.

The task of selecting your raw material is as easy as it would first appear. Every time you take a thinning flake off you lose width, so working backwards from your finished tool size, adequate allowance must be made for all the processes in achieving the required thickness ratio. A fairly sizeable nodule is therefore required and finding one of good quality can be quite difficult.

Assuming, however, that you are successful, your starting point is an analysis of your nodule. They say that great sculptors like Leonardo da Vinci could see their work inside the block of stone and it was just a matter of releasing it. This may be true or not but the thought process that is required is akin to this statement, as you must be able to 'see' your finished item to work out your reduction pattern.

The nodule will have, unless it is spherical, a longer axis and looking at it three dimensionally, it is possible to plan the width axis and the thickness. With this thought in mind you must seek a way to remove as much of the unwanted material as possible. There is no great rush about this; take your time, as removing smaller flakes takes longer but is a much safer proposition. Look for natural platforms and when you find them, see if they are abraded sufficiently for a flake removal. Far too often people rush into flaking and thereby make difficulties for later on in the process. If it helps, get a felt-tip pen and draw on your nodule by putting in the axis centre line, which will show you the masses that need to be eliminated.

Dips or cavities can often occur in a nodule so try and work out your reduction strategy to remove these obstacles before you start knapping. The first thing is to remove the masses and if possible work the ends of the nodule. If you thin the central portion first, the likelihood of breaking the nodule in half increases when you try and remove material from the ends at a later stage. Also, by removing unwanted material first, the shape you are trying to achieve will appear.

When working a large piece, there is always the problem of 'end shock'. The technique is to support as much of the nodule as possible. If you are working one end, try and support the other end on your knee with your hand or arm. End shock is always a surprise and to have a nodule over 50cm long on your knee and to tap one end and have the other end fall off takes some believing, but it can and does happen!

The tendency is to hit the nodule too quickly – stop and make sure of your angles and ensure that the platform is strong enough. If unsure, abrade the platform; think before hitting and then and only then make your strike forcefully and with sufficient power. The nodule must fracture but repeated hitting will, as we have said before, only create multiple fractures inside the flint and eventually crumble the platform.

Assuming you have removed a successful flake from approximately where you wanted it, check the scar to see if there are any flaws that might affect subsequent flakes and also if you are creating a suitable platform to progress to the next flake in your strategy. From now on each platform must be abraded, every time and without fail! I know this seems time consuming but clean fractures are important and care at these early stages are crucial. You may think that I am overly emphasising this aspect of the reduction but by this stage in your knapping you will have made lots of mistakes and realise that thinning is a careful, precise process and there are no shortcuts.

When you have removed much of the unwanted mass, take time to try and work a zigzag flaking around the centre line of your major axis with peaks above and below centre.

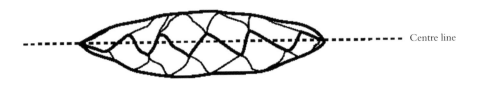

Centre line

Attempt to get a zigzag edge to the biface to create
platforms above and below the centre line.

Part-worked biface.

Now the thinning process can begin. Always look for the platform below the centre line before you strike it and if it is not below the centre line, then reverse the piece and nibble the platform to move it away from the centre line. Turn the piece back over and you will see that the platform has moved downwards. Abrade it again and then strike. This time the blow must be at an acute angle to the platform so that the flake will carry into the biface as far as possible. A short sharp blow is the best technique and can be assisted by pressing the percussor against the face before hitting, so the blow is slightly inwards rather than straight down.

One of the things that will assist in the removal of thinning flakes is to have the holding hand at 180 degrees to the hammer and to slightly pull the underside with your finger, which will help the flake to separate. Each time you work the edge to lower or raise the platform you will lose width, so get the most from your thinning flakes. Try to find ridges that extend into the biface to run further thinning flakes along.

Again, always work the ends of the biface first before removing material from the middle, as it is easier and prevents end shock. The thinner your biface becomes, the more likely that end shock will happen.

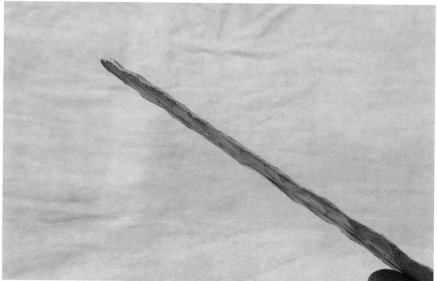

Although this is a resin replica (seen face on, and side on), it was taken from the magical 12 to 1 blade made from flint. The thinning process here is virtually impossible to replicate as the blade itself is so slender; but thinning flakes still reach past the centre of the blade.

It may be a good time to revisit the idea of the Hertzian cone and to add a little more detail. The cone itself will be approximately 100 degrees in angular structure. This means that if you strike at any position, the angle of the cone will be 50 degrees each side of the strike line, so it should be possible to assess the angle needed to hit your flint to create a perfect thinning flake.

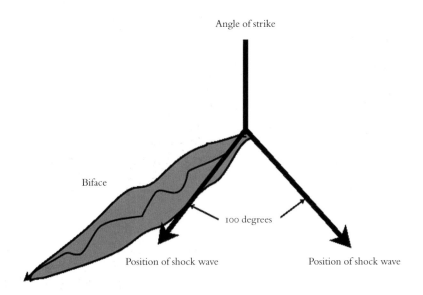

Angle of strike

Biface

100 degrees

Position of shock wave   Position of shock wave

By correctly angling the strike on a platform lower than the centre line, you can produce the perfect thinning flake.

The Hertzian cone.

The understanding of this attribute of fracture will greatly enhance your ability to perform the more delicate aspects of knapping. Knowing where the cone of fracture will happen requires the skill to assess the angle of attack and the ability to strike where you are aiming for. An aid may well be to make a 100-degree template, as this will give the exact angle of strike when it is offered up to the tool being made. After a while you will be able to make an assessment of the correct angle but using this template whilst learning can be very advantageous.

Do not forget that the angle between the hammer and the flint can have several variables when assessing the angle of strike. The flint can be moved backwards and forwards across the knee as well as down the side of the knee and rotated left and right in the hand. The downward angle of the strike can be varied and the wrist rotated to a certain degree. If the flint is held just in the hand, then it can be tipped up and down and rotated. The strike itself can be in a straight line or on a curved path and can vary in strength and length of strike. The secret is to experiment as much as possible to ascertain what advantages can be obtained and to understand the disadvantages.

Returning to the thinning of the biface, as the platforms get smaller and less material needs to be removed, it is desirable to change the size of the hammer to a smaller and lighter one. At this stage the platforms are also smaller and

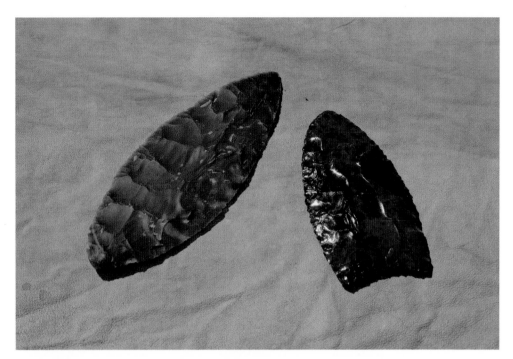

1 Flint biface made by Ed Mosher at 10 to 1 and a mahogany biface at 8 to 1. Note the flaking marks from the thinning process.

2 Fluted Clovis and Folsom points. These are modern replications but very accurate representations.

3 *A beautifully rendered piece of memorabilia made by Kurt Phillips of Oregon and a gift to the author on his tour of America. The blade, the beadwork and the knotting all made by Kurt are a lovely example of a master modern knapper.*

4 *Three bifaces made of different materials. On the left is chalcedony, the right dacite – one of the rhyolite group of igneous rocks – and the middle biface is made of flint.*

5 *Three bifaces. Lower left is basalt, lower right snowflake obsidian and the top is made from Norfolk flint from the Brandon area.*

6 A series of arrowheads from exotic USA materials: jasper, alibates, fossilised wood, novaculite and types of flint.

7 Bifaces of 8 to 1 reduction and a hand axe made from mookaite, novaculite and flint.

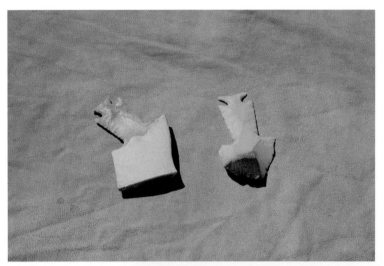

8 Some of the work by George Eklund with the sword in the stone connection. These are fun pieces and show the skill of this flint knapper.

9 These strange replica Marden points, named for a British archaeological site, have raised eyebrows in both archaeological and knapping circles due to their unusual asymmetric shape and their difficulty to manufacture. The point on the left was made by Phil Churchill and the one on the right by Jack Hemphill. If there was ever a challenge in knapping this is it, and anyone who thinks they have the skill should try to make one of these points.

10 Some of the beautiful rock materials now available on the knapping market that create a work of art rather than a functional arrowhead.

11 A series of elongated points made from black and mahogany obsidian. Each of these items were pressure flaked from a cut slab and notched in various ways to make art forms.

12 Various shapes of obsidian points and a basalt biface. The heart-shaped obsidian exotic was made by Brian Thompson.

13 *Three archaeological finds and a modern replication show that not all arrowheads are large. Note the scale in centimetres with these finds as the 'bird points' found in Missouri on the White River are almost too small to use. Nevertheless, they are genuine artefacts and were used.*

14 *Four genuine archaeological finds from the American Midwest. Found on an expedition to the banks of the White River in Missouri courtesy of Derek Mclean, the author was pleased to add these to his collection.*

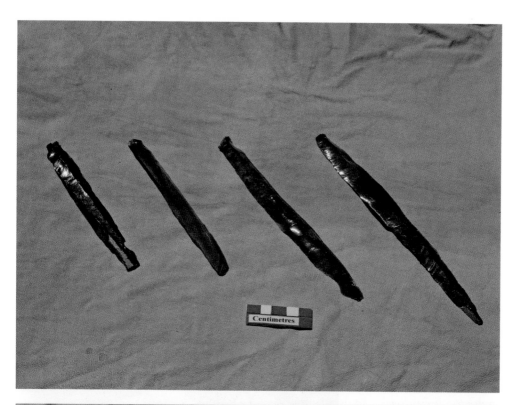

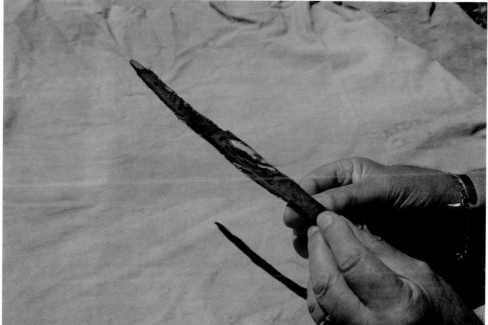

15 & 16 These spectacular blades were made by Jerry Marcantel of Tucson, Arizona and removed from an obsidian core with a large double-handed ishi stick. The sheer size of these blades is remarkable considering they were removed by pressure flaking. The side view shows the thinness of the blade, the longest of which is a fraction under 22cm. The remarkable thing is that although the core was prepared, Jerry does not prepare a platform, just taking blade after blade from a flat top core surface.

17 Beautiful Norfolk flint hand axe made for the author by Will Lord.

18 The author with a truly magnificent dance blade made from obsidian. 'As you can see from the picture I was totally mesmerised by the sheer size of this thing. A fantastic piece of American art.'

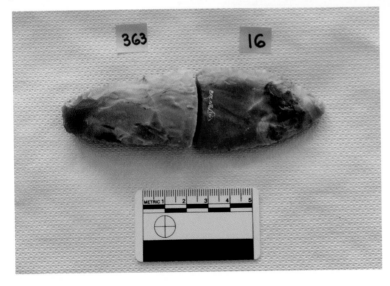

19 Found on two separate occasions, this is a type 1 dagger and was recovered from Brinsbury archaeological site and is Beaker period dated from the end of the Neolithic to the start of the Bronze Age. (Reproduced by kind permission of Chichester College Brinsbury Campus)

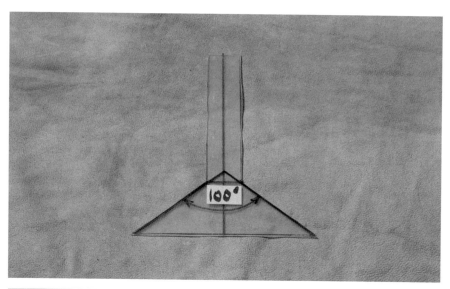

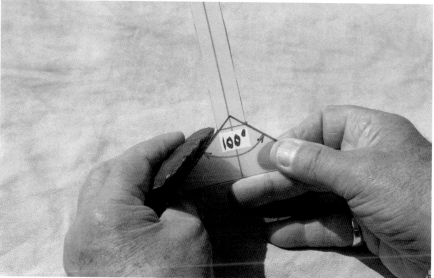

The template shows the 100-degree shape of the Hertzian pressure cone and how to use it to gauge the angle of attack and produce the perfect thinning flake.

require less abrading. It now becomes crucial to move the platform below the centre line and abrade before every strike, as at this point it becomes easier to crush a platform.

A search of the Internet will reveal a number of videos showing thinning examples but all of them will not be exactly the same. Individual preferences start to come into play as knappers develop their own skills. Some knappers lightly touch the area of flake removal, others add a slight pull with the finger, while some leave the area of flake removal completely unsupported. Again it is a matter of trial and error and to see what works for you. Another technique that will help is the 'isolated platform', which gives even more strength to the platform and allows easier removal of the flake. When preparing the platform, turn the piece upside down and remove a tiny nibbled flake from each side of the platform. This makes it stand out and gives the thinning flake a chance to start its fracture.

From personal experience, I have learned the hard way that this is a time not to be rushed. Analyse your flint, select and prepare the platform, and always abrade. Go slowly and do not try to remove too much material on your strike. Caution is the key word, as a mistake at this juncture means several hours' work can be lost. The art of successful thinning does not come automatically and you have to persevere, but the results are well worth the effort when finally achieved.

One of the arts in knapping, when you become proficient, is recognising when to stop. You can never reach perfection, as there is always one more ridge you could work. This is especially true if you have not followed the rules and allowed the middle section to become thinner than the ends or just one end. This is almost impossible to rectify without risking snapping the tool into two pieces.

The alternative is to work from a prepared slab. If you possess a rock saw with a diamond blade you can cut up your own rocks into slabs, or you can purchase ready cut slabs on the Internet.

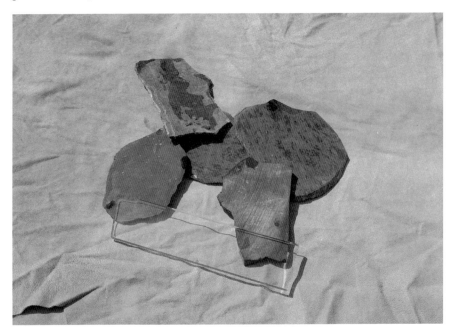

Various slabs saw cut for pressure flaking. Two types of obsidian (mahogany and snowflake), novaculite and glass.

One of the best tools for preparing rock is the electric tile cutter that you can find in most DIY shops. You may have to substitute the tile blade for a diamond blade but diamond cutting wheels are not that expensive and do last a long time. The limiting factor with a tile cutter is that the maximum cut is only about 1½cm the height of the cutting wheel which is fixed above the table. Also the safety cover limits the thickness that can be passed beneath it. A word of safety here, please be sensible as serious accidents can happen if you try to change the configuration of this powerful tool.

What it can do safely is cut up your slabs into strips or preformed shapes for pressure flaking or percussion. If you are cutting strips from a slab, make them about 5cm or 6cm wide to begin with. For percussion you will have to prepare the edges for knapping, as you need to start making the cross section elliptical. Begin by making an oblique strike on the very edge of the slab. When you have removed the first tiny flake, reverse the slab and use this scar as a platform to take another flake. Keep reversing after every removal and work the length of the slab to produce the zigzag edge as shown before. Work the other edge of the slab and then the ends. Abrade the edges and use the peaks and troughs of the zigzag as platforms to remove short flakes from the surfaces. Short flakes are required to start the elliptical cross section process. Do not worry if the flakes do not carry to the centre of the slab and you leave an area of un-knapped surface, as this will be knapped on the second pass. Once the whole slab has been pressure flaked all round, then you need to abrade it before trying to remove further flakes.

A second pass, taking flakes from the platforms below the centre line, will usually mean longer flakes, as they will follow the ridges from the first pass. If your flakes are not becoming longer, this is because you are not pressure flaking with sufficient force or are not getting the flaking angle correct.

Again refer to the notes on flaking angles and, if using your leg muscles, ensure that the flaking angle is as near to the horizontal as possible. Try varying the angle and the pressure of flaking time and time again, until you do succeed in elongating your flakes.

Slabs can be knapped by percussion as well as pressure flaking and again it is up to you which method you prefer. Many knappers use a mixture of percussion up to a certain stage and then finish with pressure flaking.

13

Let's Make an Arrowhead

I wonder how many people have read the contents page and have fast-forwarded to this section, as everyone wants to make an arrowhead. If you have, then you are in for a shock, as there is no shortcut. You have to learn all the lessons on how to knap before you can produce even a passable finished tool.

Firstly, let us think about what an arrowhead is and what it is used for. An arrowhead is a tool for cutting as many blood vessels as possible in the killing process. Unless you are lucky enough to hit a major artery with your shot that would almost instantly kill your prey, then the penetration of the arrowhead would cause some internal bleeding. Even if the prey had been shot with a number of arrows, it could still continue its escape for quite a way until the loss of blood took its toll. An arrowhead therefore needs to be sharp on all its cutting edges and thin enough to allow maximum penetration.

The thinness of an arrowhead is also necessary to allow it to be shafted. Spears can be quite substantial but an arrow must be light enough to be shot from a bow and balanced to be aerodynamically stable. Arrowheads can be manufactured from a flake, a prepared core and a slab so let us look in detail at all three.

Many arrowheads are beautifully made and the fully worked barbed and tanged arrowhead with full bifacial flaking is a thing of beauty.

Five of the cache of over eighty arrowheads that were recovered from Brinsbury archaeological site; they are Beaker period – dating from the end of the Neolithic to the start of the Bronze Age. The site produced a mixture of Conygar Hill, Green Low and Sutton types of arrowheads. (Reproduced by kind permission of Chichester College Brinsbury Campus)

To be functional, however, the arrowhead does not have to be carefully finished, as long as it conforms to the criteria already discussed. The finished product will perform well without full flaking but can look quite rough and not so aesthetically pleasing. Arrowheads may well have been used as barter currency, as many are found in perfect condition.

A series of functional arrowheads made from novaculite, flint and chalcedony. Not all arrowheads were beautifully made barbed and tanged masterpieces. Many were functional and were made quickly, possibly for a one-off use. These examples show how fast and still effective an arrowhead could be made.

First we will look at using a flake to make an arrowhead. While you have been knapping many flakes have been removed that are suitable for further working, but they have one drawback, that being the bulb of percussion. If the flake is sufficiently large enough, the bulb end can be broken off or, if prepared correctly with a platform, it can be partly removed with percussion. This leaves you with a feathering flake that can be pressure flaked by using the side of the pressure flaker to make a pointed end. Light pressure flaking abruptly taken along the edges will produce a working arrowhead almost instantly. If a larger or thicker flake is used, then the edges can be invasively pressure flaked to produce a far more pleasing finished item. As a recap, the abrupt and the invasive pressure flake is determined solely by the angle of attack, so a mixture of techniques will give the required results. Abrupt flaking when abraded will make an ideal platform for an invasive flake.

The notching technique allows easier attachment to an arrow shaft, as there is then something to wind twine or sinew around when attaching the point to the shaft. To notch successfully you need a sharpened pressure flaker of less diameter than the notch slot width. Hold it at 90 degrees to the edge of the workpiece and press straight down, removing a small flake. Turn the flint over and repeat the process, again at 90 degrees, in the scar left by the previous flake removal. Each time you take a flake, rotate the arrowhead and use the last flake scar, but try not to remove too much material at each go. Take it slowly and carefully and work into the body of the arrowhead and you will find that a slot will form.

Arrowhead blanks.

Again be warned that any sideways pressure will break bits off the side of the slot. Always use pressure at 90 degrees or you will break the arrowhead. Also, if your pressure flaker widens out too far, you will be exerting sideways pressure, this time from the flaker being wider than the slot.

Do not try and make an arrowhead from a flake that is very thin, as the slightest error in flaking will break the piece. It really is a matter of trial and error, so try using flakes of all shapes and sizes until you find a successful method of your own.

A prepared core is an excellent way to produce perfectly formed arrowheads but in this case utilise the Levallois process, explained earlier. Low profile radial flaking will produce a flattened dome shape and then by reversing the core and striking as if taking off a rejuvenation flake, you can produce the perfect arrowhead blank.

The blank must now be flaked into a rough shape using the side of the flaker and then abraded. The action of grinding will produce a lowered platform that is suitable for invasive pressure flaking. When one side is complete, repeat the grinding process to lower the platform on the other side of the arrowhead and then pressure flake this side as well. Abrupt flaking will then straighten the edges and sharpen them. Before the final pass of flaking, make the slots between the barbs and the tang but do not forget to remove really sharp edges around the tang so that they do not cut into the binding when the arrowhead is mounted.

Possibly the easiest, and of course the most modern method, is to make an arrowhead from a prepared slab that can either be rectangular or an arrowhead shape. Ensure the sides of the slab are well abraded to allow the pressure flaker to grip the edge and invasively work both sides to produce an elliptical cross

Conygar Hill type

Barbs same length or
shorter than the tang
and the base is either
concave or flat.

Sutton type

Some have no
barbs or very
tiny barbs and
the arrowhead is
usually under 8g in
weight.

Greenlow type

Barbs are always
longer than the
tang and the base
is concave.

Ballyclare type

Similar to the
Sutton but far
chunkier and with
a weight of more
than 8g.

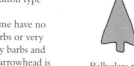

Kilmarnock type

Pointed barbs that
are shorter than the
tang and some with
no barbs.

Barbed and tanged arrowheads.

section. If the slab is thin, then the arrowhead can be completed with almost a single pass but usually a second or even a third pass is required. This thins the slab and also provides the required cross section. If working from a rectangle, then after the first pass, abruptly cut down the edge to produce the arrow shape, abrade and then take further invasive passes. This may have to be done several times. If you are working with a triangular preformed shape, then the base needs to be invasively pressure flaked, otherwise the material will not be thin enough to allow slots to be made for forming the barbs and tang.

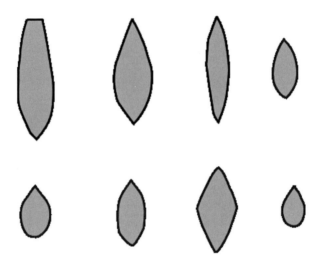

There is a whole range of leaf-shaped arrowheads ranging from short and squat to long and slender.

Made from flakes with invasive retouch they follow the flake shape and are diverse with twelve different categories.

Laurel leaf arrowheads.

There are not many varieties of barbed and tanged arrowheads in the UK, as they belong to a very short period at the end of the Neolithic and the beginning of the Bronze Age. This period covered a few hundred years when metal was slowly being introduced.

Before this period arrowheads were of the 'laurel leaf' type.

The laurel leaf arrowhead is made in a similar way to the barbed and tanged but by using a blade rather than a flake, or the modern approach, the slab.

When working flint, knappers usually have difficulty in making pressure flakes travel across the arrowhead, so that the flake scars look more abrupt than invasive. This problem can only be rectified by increasing the pressure or altering the angle of attack, whichever is causing the trouble. Pressure flaking usually requires a certain amount of upper-body strength and if you cannot exert sufficient force, then you must revert to the use of leg power to increase pressure, as shown earlier. The fact is that your legs are far more robust than any other muscles in the body as they carry you around all day, but using leg power is difficult to master so it is advisable to revisit the technique.

For right-handed people, hold the pressure flaker in your right hand and the flint in your left on the slotted or the soft pad. It is crucial that the attack angle is directed into the workpiece in such a way as to get the maximum length of flake.

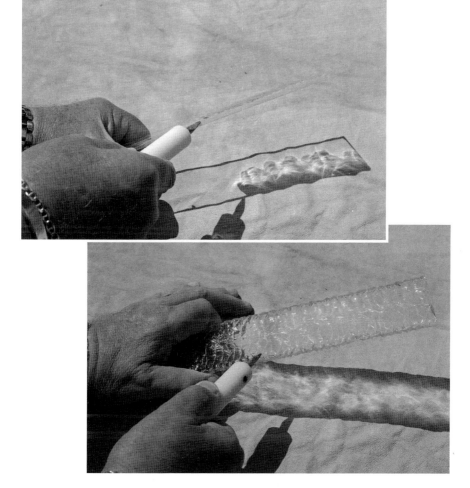

Where to put the flaker on the slab: the contact should be 25mm into the slab and 75–100mm from the previous point of contact. After making the flake shape like the Nile delta, it should be straightened out so the next flake can run parallel to the previous flake. To do this, take a tiny flake out to straighten the side of this delta shape.

The pad needs to be held at an angle that allows the flaking tool to be placed on the workpiece and then the wrist is turned, so the pad is parallel to the ground. In this position you will not be able to see the actual point of contact, as it will be hidden by the rotated pad. The backs of both of your hands should be on the insides of your knees and by closing your legs, the leg muscles add to the pressure being exerted by your arm muscles.

To start with you will find it extremely difficult to achieve the correct position so study the photographs. It feels very awkward at first to work in this way, as you tend to forget that you are using your leg muscles, and also to turn the pad to the horizontal position. Only by practice will this position become second nature. You can tell if you are successful immediately by the sound that you hear as the flake gives way. It is a sharp crack and should result in a greatly elongated flake.

One of the best materials to start with is glass, as it is much easier to work than flint and with practice you will be able to run a pressure flake up to 4cm without too much effort.

Remember that initially you will put a lot of effort into pressure flaking until you have managed to master the technique and will become easily tired, as you are using muscles in an unfamiliar way. Take frequent breaks, especially if you are feeling pressure in your shoulders, but once you are used to pressure flaking it becomes much easier as you allow your legs to do the work.

The technique is the same for using a hand-held pressure flaker or an elongated ishi stick. With the long pressure flaker, you just tuck the shaft under your arm as in the photographs.

Recap

The book so far has shown you the way to produce and replicate the tools of the Palaeolithic to the Bronze Age. We have also strayed into the realms of the modern knapper by the use of copper tools and making items from slab material. Purists will want to use only the tools of the period – that of the hammer stone, the antler hammer, the antler tine for pressure flaking and the fabricator. This is fine as there is a great deal to be said for knapping using only what was available then and personal choice is what knapping is all about.

For those who wish to be more adventurous and use today's tools and techniques, all well and good, as we will be going into areas where traditional tools are inadequate for the tasks.

By now you should be an accomplished knapper and be able to replicate many of the tools of the periods you are interested in. You will have mastered to some extent the ability to thin by percussion and to pressure flake, so we have reached the point where we can move onwards and look in detail at other parts of the world where knapping has far exceeded the tool types that we find in the British Isles.

14

AN INTRODUCTION TO AMERICAN KNAPPING

Looking at other areas of the world where flint was used to make tools, Europe, particularly France, Germany, the Low Countries and especially Denmark provide a great wealth of material. The problem with the northern part of Europe is that in the last million years the land has only been suitable for occupation for about 30 per cent of the time. For the majority of that period the whole area was a polar desert due to the coming and going of ice ages but further south the climatic changes were not so severe so the land was occupied for longer periods. Central and southern France and the area of northern Spain have produced a wealth of flint artefacts and many museums are worth a visit to see the beautiful array of tools from many periods.

The areas of France and Spain are especially rich in Neanderthal tools. The Solutrean technology, named after the site of Solutré discovered in 1886, in the Macon region of eastern France, appeared around 21,000 years ago, when Britain was still locked in the Devensian Ice Age. The industry followed the Mousterian period and artefacts found include flint tools, ornamental beads, bone pins as well as prehistoric art.

Solutrean tool-making employed techniques not seen before in Europe and produced finely worked bifacial points made with percussion reduction and pressure flaking rather than the cruder knapping of the previous periods. Knapping was done using antler, wood batons and soft stone hammers that permitted the working of delicate flint removal, whilst pressure flaking produced a final finish.

Large thin spearheads have been found, some with tang and shoulder on one side only, as well as end scrapers, knives and denticulate saws. All are beautifully knapped. The industry first appeared in Spain but disappeared from the archaeological record around 17,000 BP, which explains why we find none of this material in Britain.

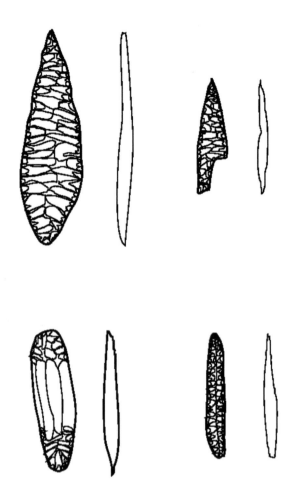

Solutrean flints.

As the Devensian Ice Age started to relent there was a migration of hunter-gatherers into Germany and southern Scandinavia starting about 12,000 years ago, slightly earlier than the migration into Britain. The sea levels were lower then, so this part of Europe was a solid land mass with Britain being a peninsular on the north edge of Europe.

The massive river system of the Thames, Rhine and Seine flowed westwards at that time, along what would eventually become the English Channel, and emptied with a huge delta near where the Scilly Isles are today. This major waterway would have been a huge barrier for direct migration from Europe and entry was restricted to a route up through eastern Germany into southern Scandinavia and across the area of the North Sea, known as 'Doggerland'. Britain was consequently an outpost of Europe and lagged behind in flint technology.

The rise of sea levels and the separation of Britain from Europe circa 6,000 years ago meant that these shores could only be reached by a sea journey.

There was a gradual transition during the Neolithic period from hunter-gatherers to farming communities and it was also the start of monument building, pottery and trade. By the end of this period and the start of the Bronze Age, new ideas were being introduced, including a change in pottery style to Beakers. These innovations coincided with the appearance of metal tools and because of their rarity, they would have been treasured possessions.

Lanceolate (from the French for 'lance shaped') flint daggers, similar to the Solutrean spear points, were being made at this time and these were being manufactured from a nodule by percussion reduction and then pressure flaking.

Lanceolate shaped dagger.

These long, thin and beautifully made daggers are commonly found in Germany, Jutland and Denmark and a few have been found in Britain. They were made by reducing a nodule to a long, thin elliptical cross section by percussion and expert thinning and then finishing with pressure flaking. As time went on, the base end of the lanceolate shape was narrowed to form a handle. It is not known if these daggers were hafted but later the 'handle' part of the dagger was thickened, taking on a triangular or square cross section.

These daggers must have been made to replicate metal ones, as later examples even suggest stitching in the flintwork to make them look like their hafted metal counterpart. A metal dagger at that time must have been a very rare and costly object for such trouble to be taken in their flint copies. As time went on, the dagger became more and more sophisticated in its manufacture and finish. Eventually, as metals became more readily available, the flint dagger fell into disuse.

Danish daggers are classified into six groups as the style developed.

Type 1
Lanceolate shape lacking
a developed handle that is
as thick as the blade.

Type 3
Similar to type 2 but
handle is square or
diamond cross section.

Type 5
Similar to type 4 but
no seam on handle.

Type 2
Lanceolate shape with
a defined handle and
oval cross section.

Type 4
Defined square or
triangular cross section
and defined pommel.

Type 6
Fairly thick handle
with almost round
cross section.

Types 1 to 6 daggers.

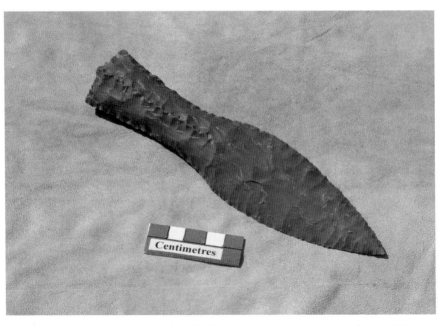

This is a modern replication by Philip Churchill of Quartzsite, Arizona. It's a type 4 dagger and shows stitching replication of the handle and the pommel. Made from flint, the handle is square and the blade wide and flat. Notice the carefully worked blade edge and especially the pommel detail. These daggers date to the end of the Neolithic, beginning of the Bronze Age in the Beaker period. Philip is a superb craftsman and, at the time of writing, has made over 1,450 of these daggers. I have had the privilege to sit and watch him make one.

In modern replication, the type 4 dagger is possibly the most popular. It has a flattened blade and a square or triangular handle with stitching replicated on the pommel and one or both sides of the handle.

To make a dagger of the same quality as shown in the picture made by Philip Churchill, you must go through a series of stages. Let me stress that a replication of this standard is only for the experienced knapper, although an approximation of the finished product is within the reach of someone with relative skills. Do have a try but do not be disappointed if the end result does not match the dagger shown. When this dagger was knapped, Philip had already made around 1,400 daggers, so he is the world's leading expert.

Stage 1
This is obviously to select your raw material. The nodule must be of quality flint and of sufficient size to allow a dagger of 20cm to 25cm to be made.

Stage 2
Remove all cortex by bifacial flaking and 'rough out' to an oval shape. Then start to aim for parallel sides and a thickness of approximately 5cm to 6cm.

Stage 3
Bearing in mind that the thickest part of the dagger is the handle, start to produce a rough-out of the finished shape with a flat base and an elliptical cross section.

Stage 4
This is a further rough-out stage, where the cross section of the blade is symmetrical and lenticular and reduced in thickness but the handle end is left slightly thicker. Be especially careful not to reduce mass from the centre portion first, as this makes the piece liable to break if you then remove mass from the ends. As a rule of knapping – always work the ends first.

Stage 5
The handle now needs to be cut in from the width, so more abrupt flaking is required to produce the cross section of the handle, be it square or triangular. If you want to attempt stitching (one side if triangular and both sides if square), there must be a definite crest or ridge on the handle cross section. That is to say, the flakes removed to give the handle its required cross section must be taken at an acute angle so that they are very abrupt and result in a sharp edge at 90 degrees to the flat of the blade on one or both sides.

Stage 6

In the final rough-out stage, where the overall shape of the dagger is made, the handle section must be parallel-sided and of the required shape and the blade section thinned to approximately the desired thickness. Care must be taken for the transition between the handle section and the blade section.

Stage 7

Where the base of the handle meets the blade section, it must be worked carefully so there is a smooth but definite junction to the transition. Also the end of the handle must be slightly flared to allow the pommel to be formed. The blade must now be thinned to almost its final thickness and then it is ready for pressure flaking or very careful percussion to get parallel uniform flakes across the blade.

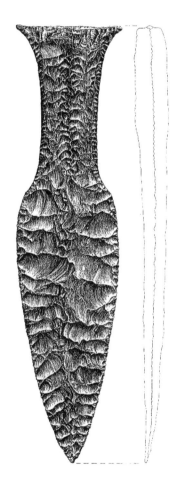

A type 4 dagger (drawn by Val Waldorf).

Stage 8
Working alternate sides, a small punch is used to make the stitching by taking uniformly tiny flakes from the handle ridge and the pommel ridge. Also the sides of the handle must be abruptly punched to make a final edge. Stitching replication may need a second pass with the punch to indent the scars left by the first.

Stage 9
Finish the blade with flaking along both edges to sharpen the blade and give a uniform look.

Stage 10
If you have managed to get this far and have produced a dagger, be very proud of your achievement and show it to all of your friends!

As has previously been said, flint is not widely available in every part of the world so local stone was used to manufacture tools. There is evidence of material being traded, sometimes with a wide distribution, but the majority of tools were made and used locally. Britain became an island about 8,000 years ago, so any trade of raw material or finished tools had to be transported across the sea, which made the use of local stone even more likely.

There is very little material in Britain of volcanic origin that can be knapped. The nearest naturally occurring obsidian is in eastern Europe and the Canary Islands. It is formed by rapid cooling of volcanic emissions and so it is not readily found of knappable quality anywhere that could be considered local to the British Isles.

The Americas, on the other hand, have vast reserves of obsidian, especially in the western states of North America and in South America. Volcanic glass is far easier to work than flint and therefore far more detailed and better-finished tools can be achieved.

Chert is also easy to work and appears in areas of limestone deposition such as central France and again the Americas.

Although in the past some wonderful worked tools have been recovered in Europe, the Far East and South America, the one place where modern knappers have taken the artefacts of their indigenous peoples a step further to the level of an art form is North America. The early American Indian finds are beautifully made with great skill and much attention to detail, but with the advent of modern knapping tools and techniques, the American knapper of today is producing tools that have far more to do with art than use.

No book on knapping would or could be complete without a detailed look at what is being produced in the USA and how it is being done.

15

AMERICAN TIME PERIODS AND TYPES OF POINTS

Following the first settlers in the Americas in the fifteenth century and the expansion into the West over the next 300 to 400 years, there was a meeting between the 'new' immigrants and a Stone Age culture. Due to the widespread myths generated by the American film industry, people outside of North America know very little of the 'first Americans', so a brief look at these people and their history and culture is needed to set the scene for an understanding of knapping US style.

The Devensian Ice Age reached its peak between 28,000 and 18,000 years ago and moved vast ice sheets into the Americas and northern Europe. Some of these ice sheets were over a mile thick and contained huge quantities of fresh water so sea levels were considerably lower. There was a land bridge between Asia and Alaska, the Grand Banks were dry land, as was the North Sea and large areas around all continents.

As the Ice Age came to an end, the temperature started to rise and areas of the northern part of the world moved from polar desert to land inhabited firstly by plants, then animals and eventually early Homo Sapiens. The arrival of the first people in the Americas is still a matter of conjecture, as very little trace is left by hunter-gatherers, save their tools, and an exact date is unknown at this time, but it is thought to be circa 16,000 years ago.

Evidence exists of a migration through an ice-free corridor from Asia across the Bering Strait and through Alaska and Canada. This migration was, in geological terms, exceedingly fast, as there is evidence for populations in the southern parts of South America by 13,000 years ago.

There is, however, a growing accumulation of evidence that the route via Alaska was not the only entry of people into the Americas. There is no evidence of long blade technology in the Americas as found in the Far East, but many of the earliest finds bear a marked resemblance to those from Europe. The first dateable finds in North America are from the Clovis people. It has been found that their spearheads are almost identical to the Solutrean finds from France and the Iberian Peninsula. This has given rise to the hypothesis that there was a migration of technology around the edge of the North Atlantic ice sheet. The lowering of sea levels could have exposed large tracts of land extending from Newfoundland to South Wales or the Bristol Channel that would make a voyage by boat, following the edge of the ice sheet, entirely possible. Inuit Indians, in the not so distant past, lived a nomadic existence under these harsh conditions.

The major problem with tracing a Stone Age culture is that there is no written record, so the only evidence available to reconstruct a long forgotten people is what they left behind. Very little would survive the ravages of time from a nomadic existence, where dwellings were made from wood or skin, except their tools.

When talking about North America you have to think about its immense size and realise that if you travelled from coast to coast, your journey would be greater than from London in the UK to Istanbul in Turkey.

Europe and North America to scale.

Consequently, there are areas in the west of this vast country where the easiest obtainable knapping rock is all volcanic, with rhyolites and obsidian predominating. The middle and eastern seaboards tend to have more of the flint and chert type rocks, which means that, although the rocks are all capable of a conchoidal fracture, there are regional differences. Another point is that the land mass is so great that archaeological sites tend to be widely distributed, as do the flora and fauna. The land mass size and altitude give a wide variety of climates, sometimes over a very short distance. Plains and grasslands stand side-by-side with mountain ranges and desert, so different species of animals and their migrations make for a wide variety to meet the needs of humans to live and survive.

The history of the Americas only spans the period from the end of the Devensian Ice Age to the present day and compared with the European archaeological record, is comparatively short. As nomadic peoples lived in many of the American periods, evidence of habitation in some areas is very scarce.

The landing of Europeans in the Americas and the subsequent colonisation of the continent between the fifteenth and nineteenth centuries greatly changed the way of life of the indigenous peoples and the advent of modern weapons meant a decline of traditional tools.

In Britain we have our way of dividing up the past, but the American system is somewhat different and can have regional differences. To show a comparison, I have taken the American Midwest of the Plains Indians as a typical example and used their chronology. The terminology will be strange to many people, especially the names of some of their tool types, but the system of recording using the place name of their first discovery still persists.

A few moments with a map of North America will show many names that are, in European eyes, very different, as some are taken from the Indian terms.

Years ago	European period	American period
12,000 BC Palaeolithic	Late Upper	Palaeo Indian
10,000 BC	Early Mesolithic	
8,000 BC	Later Mesolithic	Early Archaic
6,000 BC		Middle Archaic
4,000 BC	Early Neolithic	
3,000 BC	Later Neolithic	Late Archaic
2,500 BC	Early Bronze Age	
1,200 BC	Late Bronze Age	
1,000 BC		Early Woodland
100 BC	Iron Age	Middle Woodland
AD 500		Later Woodland
AD 1200		Mississippian

Where the major use of stone tools in Europe was coming to an end by the Iron Age, in the Americas the coming of metal was a gradual process that started in the east by AD 1500, but further west changes were as late as AD 1800 from migration westwards. Metal was also introduced from the south from Spanish sources, but again the transition was gradual.

Once the Americas were settled and farmed, stone tools started to turn up as the land was ploughed consisting of many thousands of projectile points from the peoples of a bygone age. Strangely, the bow and arrow did not come into use until around AD 700 in the Woodland period, even though the earlier finds were termed 'points'. The use of these tools was as diverse as their European counterparts and consisted of a full toolkit for hunting, food preparation and farming.

Many tools like scrapers, piercers, drills and burins, to name just a few, abound from archaeological sites, as do axes and adzes, but the predominant finds are arrowheads. Knives and projectile points all seemingly come under the term 'point'. Modern-day knapping appears to be limited to these finds only, and as the spear point and the knife could be one and the same, especially when they are serrated, little distinction is made as to their use.

Apart from fluting, which seems to be predominant in the early periods, the method of production was the same as the European toolkit. The flute was an elongated flake taken longitudinally on both sides of the point at right angles to the previous flaking.

Stage 2
Prepare a platform on the concave bottom edge.

Stage 3
Strike the flute from the point.

Stage 4
Rotate the point.

Stage 5
Repeat the process on the second side.

Stage 1
Prepare a fully flaked point with a concave lower edge.

Point of contact.

Fluted point.

There is a great debate running currently in the United States about the earliest peoples. The accepted earliest group are termed 'Clovis' people from circa 11,000 to 9,000 BC. However, there is growing evidence of finds that seem to predate the Clovis period, although this has not yet been totally accepted by the archaeological establishment. There appears to have been a much earlier and more primitive culture that produced cruder stone tools, but we must await further evidence to add support to this speculation.

The variety and size of American projectile points is vast, as each 'tribe' seemed to manufacture their own type of point according to their specific needs. Small arrowheads of just over a centimetre long were made, as well as long points of up to 60cm and above. The latter, called 'dance blades', were likely to have been for ceremonial purposes as they were too unwieldy for common use.

For illustration purposes, I have concentrated on the point types of the American Midwest. There are over 1,600 different variations of points from across the United States and Canada. Some are quite localised but examples from the Midwest show a variation of types that give an idea of just how extensive the finds are from American archaeology.

As there are so many point variations, I have tried to give an example from each period to show the diversity of finds. This list is by no means comprehensive but by attempting to copy some of these points, you will improve your skill as a knapper and give variety to your collection.

Clovis: 11,000 BC to 9,000 BC

These blades, closely resembling the European Solutrean, are found across the whole of North America and are very distinctive by the fluting on both sides of the blade. The flutes are single or multiple detachments from the base of the blade and this type of point was used extensively for hunting large prey, including mastodon and mammoth as well as smaller animals. They are extremely well made with a base that is concave with grounded sides so they could easily be attached to spears.

The point is made by percussion to thin the nodule or equally it could be made from a thick blade. The end is prepared by concave reduction of the base and leaving a platform for the flute, then further concave reduction and a platform on the other side for the second flute.

Clovis blade.

Folsom: 9,000 BC to 8,000 BC

This fine and delicate blade exhibits a huge flute on both sides running the length of the point and the edges are finely worked by pressure flaking. They appear to be found only on the high plains, the semi-arid deserts of the western States. The flute makes this a totally distinctive blade, as its width extends almost all the way across the blade. These points were used almost exclusively for the hunting of an early species of bison and are extremely rare finds in other parts of the States as their use was very specific.

To make this point the rough-out must be thinner than the Clovis type and the flute must travel almost the full length of the blade.

Folsom point.

Cumberland: 8,500 BC to 7,900 BC

This is more widely found throughout the south-eastern States. These points are identical to the fluted Cumberland but obviously have no fluting preparation. They have a recurved shape that narrows towards the concave base with a well-made point and has distinctive outspread 'ears'.

When making this point, the narrowing of the sides towards the base could pose problems because if you cut into the sides, you could ruin the elliptical shape. The reduction is made by thinning flakes so that the cross section of the point is the same throughout its length.

Cumberland.

Dalton: 8,500 BC to 7,900 BC

This is one of the more popular points for replication. The Dalton is found across all of the Great Plains and the south-eastern States and is a point that has the characteristics of the earlier Clovis with thinning in the hafting area and quite often sharpened by bevelling. It can also be serrated and may well have had a secondary use as a knife. The fluting is made with very short flakes and the base of the point is reduced in width to make prominent 'ears'.

Making this point is much like the Clovis, although the cross section can be somewhat thicker. The serration is done last of all with a very sharp pressure

flaker by taking evenly spaced material with
a vertical notch, the same as in notched point
making. Many knappers do this using a horseshoe nail mounted in a handle.

Dalton.

Hardaway Side Notched: 8,000 BC to 7,000 BC

This is a short stubby point with a concave base with side notches that seem
to give the barbs an upward pointed look. Found mainly in the south-west of
the States, this is the first known point to have side notches.

This is one of the easier points to make, as it is quite
thick and can be made from a flake. Care must be
taken when producing the side notches so as not to
sever the 'ears'.

Hardaway.

Agate Basin: 8,500 BC to 7,400 BC

This long, slender lanceolate point tapers gradually from the base and the flaking by percussion was done with great care to achieve parallel flaking. The
point is found extensively across the Midwest and the Great Plains and was
used for hunting deer and bison.

Made from the reduction of a nodule, these points are quite thick in comparison with other points of the period.
The base tends to be flat or slightly
convex and the widest part is about two-
thirds of the way up the point.

Agate Basin.

Hardin: 8,000 BC to 5,500 BC

This point is found across the prairie areas of the Midwest and is as thick as the Agate Basin and the same width but not so elongated. The point tapers quite quickly and at the base there are distinctive large notches that give the point a double barbed appearance. It is usually made with quite large reduction flaking that gives the edges a slightly serrated look.

The base is quite thick and slightly concave, with the base 'ears' not so prominent as the secondary 'ears'. The notches between the 'ears' are done with large flake removals that extend to the centre of the point.

Hardin.

Thebes: 8,000 BC to 6,000 BC

This is a short stubby point with massive side notches. Found throughout the Midwest, this thick, cumbersome point is sharpened with secondary flaking along its edges and the base is tapered and slightly concave. It has the appearance of being roughly made and then delicately flaked along the cutting edges.

The side notches are quite hard to make, as the elliptical shape thickens quite considerably, so a good deal of force is required to make the notch.

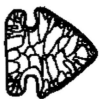

Thebes.

Pine Tree: 7,500 BC to 6,800 BC

Looking very much like a rocket ship, this point flares out towards the base giving it a totally distinctive shape. The tip area has an abrupt shoulder and the base is flat with small 'ears'. The side 'ears' produced from the notching are quite substantial and have distinctive squared corners. Made from a nodule, the flaking is finely done and a secondary pass is used to sharpen the edges. Great care must be taken with the tip, as it is very sharp and liable to break.

Pine Tree.

Rice Lobed: 7,500 BC to 6,500 BC

With a distinctive base, this thick but quite large point is often found re-
sharpened, which may indicate a possible multi-use tool. One of the earliest
bifuricated base types, it is found in the central
Midwest and has a somewhat rough appearance.

Rice lobed.

Susquehanna: 1,700 BC to 1,500 BC

This is mainly confined to the northern part of the Midwest. This broad
blade with a narrowing neck is distinguished by a wide notch and
a concave base. Again, the thickness is substantial but
narrows with almost straight sides to the tip.

Susquehanna.

Turkey-tail: 1,500 BC to 500 BC

This is a very large point with a most unusual base and bulging sides. The tip
is in the shape of a slight recurve and the point itself is sharpened with abrupt
flaking on all its edges. Common across most of
the Midwest, Turkey-tails in various forms were
traded in other areas of the States.

Turkey-tail.

Snyder: 200 BC to AD 200

There are many different forms of Snyder points but all are broad and squat with substantial notches. Made on blades, they can have an almost flat profile with retouched edges to produce an elliptical shape. They are made with large flaking towards the centre and abrupt flaking along the edges including the notches.

Snyder.

Cahokia: AD 900 to AD 1,150

Named after the Cahokia Mounds site just outside of St Louis, these distinctive triangular points are found throughout the Midwest, south-east and the Great Plains. These ugly small points with flat bases and side notches are associated with the mound builders of the Mississippi and Ohio valleys.

Cahokia.

These are just a few of the 1,600 different point types found in the United States and are by no means a comprehensive listing.

16

Is There a Connection Between European and American Knapping?

There is obviously a connection but you have to remember that the two cultures had completely different backgrounds and land masses, as well as landscapes, fauna and flora and weather conditions.

European knapping goes back over a million years so there is a heritage of knapping, whilst American knapping has only been around for roughly 14,000 to 16,000 years according to present-day knowledge.

The diversity of American projectile points also shows just how different local conditions were, as tools were made for specific uses. Spears, knives and arrowheads were all manufactured to suit the needs of the people, so those living on the wide-open plains required different tool types from those living in woodland.

Having said all this, the variations of projectile points must fall within certain parameters, as the tool type was designed for killing and rendering.

Until about 150 years ago the possibility that man had been around for more than a few thousand years was never contemplated. In Britain, the famous Archbishop Usher's statement that the world was created on 23 March 4,004 BC was widely believed. The discovery of diluvial animals led people to believe that there had been several episodes of Creation that accounted for the extinction of species. Flint and stone tools have been recovered in Britain since 1690, when a spear head was found in association with elephant remains. This was explained at the time as the remains of a battle between Iron Age warriors and Roman invaders with elephants!

In the late eighteenth century, flint implements were described as belonging 'to a very ancient period indeed even before that of the present world'. Needless to say, this was not accepted in academic circles. It was not until the early nineteenth century that with the quantity of finds recovered, there was acceptance for 'antiquity' being pushed further and further back.

By 1860 the science of geology opened up the idea of 'great antiquity', as evidence of ice sheets and geological deposition of sedimentary rocks gained ground. Also at this time the discoveries of Cro-Magnon skeletal remains in the south of France added weight to the argument of a much earlier Creation. Some of the first finds were termed 'Eoliths', which were very simple pebble stones with some sharp edges. The debate as to whether Eoliths are humanly struck tools or accidents of nature has never been satisfactorily resolved.

The stone tools in Britain may now be dated back as far as 950,000 years but further discoveries are still being made. The first flint tools discovered in association with 'humans' were found at the site of Boxgrove in West Sussex and dated circa 495,000 years ago.

The Boxgrove hand axe or biface is always a popular task for the knapper to replicate.

For the accomplished knapper, the Boxgrove biface is a relatively easy task. Although they were well made, the tool was functional rather than decorative.

Further discoveries in the twentieth century have now given us an exceedingly good picture of what happened during the last million years. Unfortunately, as Britain lies mostly above 51 degrees north, the record of 'human' activity is far from complete, as each Ice Age turned even the South Coast into a polar desert and Britain was only inhabited about 30 per cent of the time. Following the Ipswichian Ice Age from 130,000 to 70,000 years ago, animals returned but there is no evidence of human re-colonisation. This may well have been because during this period, Britain briefly became an island following a rise in sea level and this may account for the gap in the finds record.

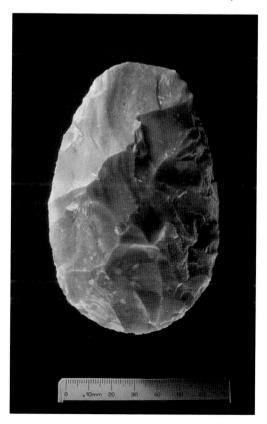

Again there is no evidence of human occupation between the interstadial of 35,000 to 40,000 years ago and 11,500 years ago but following the end of the Devensian Ice Age, there are signs of re-colonisation during the period of the Late Upper Palaeolithic.

One of the many hand axes recovered from the Boxgrove dig in West Sussex led by Mark Roberts and Matt Pope. (Reproduced with grateful thanks to the Boxgrove Project)

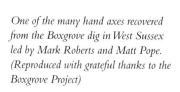

We have looked in previous chapters at the periods up to the Bronze Age when metal was introduced. Britain by this time was an island so the influx of 'new' technology always tended to lag behind the rest of Europe. With the advent of copper then bronze and finally iron, the use of flint tools diminished and would only really be revived in the relatively modern era with the need for gun flints.

The Americas were, however, different. There seems to be no direct evidence of the land being populated until the Devensian Ice Age released its grip on the continent. This started to happen earlier than in Britain when the melt waters from the Laurentian Shield and Canada changed the salinity of the North Atlantic and moved the Gulf Stream further south. As the climate in Britain is very much tied to the Gulf Stream, this continuation of the Ice Age was called the 'Younger Dryas Period' and lasted for about 400 to 500 years.

The migration into North America was either by water along the edge of the ice front or via an ice-free corridor through Alaska and Canada. The Bering Strait was dry land at that time as sea levels were much lower. The date of this migration or maybe several migrations is unknown, but it probably took place somewhere between 16,000 and 13,000 years ago.

We have also discussed the possible introduction of stone tool technology from Europe but whatever the truth is of the early colonisation of the Americas, the culture was still that of a primitive people.

As the land mass was so vast, the population would have been very scattered. At first there would have been small isolated groups of hunter-gatherers, probably extended families that eventually became larger groups or tribes. Later, some tribes formed larger settlements and adopted a more sedentary life as farming communities. This lifestyle developed in many areas, especially in the Midwest in the Mississippi and Ohio valleys with the large communities of 'mound builders', but their culture was still primitive.

It was not until contact with 'outside' cultures that changes came about with the introduction of new ideas. The Vikings have been acknowledged with contact round about the eleventh century but had little or no impact on the indigenous population, and it was not until the 1400s that the first real contact was made with Europeans in the East and a little later, the South West by the Spanish.

The spread of European ideas and new technology into Middle America was a very slow process and it would take at least 300 to 400 years before this was fully attained. The major impact on the indigenous people was not just the European way of life but also the introduction of the technology of metal.

The term 'flint' in the Americas is a term that covers not just geological flint but all knappable stone. Various local stones were used and especially volcanic rocks found in the western part of the country.

American archaeology was very slow to get going and it was not until the middle of the last century that flint replication started.

There is a great displacement of time between the Old World and the New but for all the reasons discussed, flint knapping history is different. In Britain we are all still replicating finds, but the American scene has taken knapping a stage further by turning it more into a work of art. The use of exotic-coloured materials in order to make a tool more eye-catching is common, as is developing the technology by making the work finer and better than the originals.

There are a large number of people involved on the American scene of knapping that far outnumber devotees in Europe. Regular knapping meetings are held all over the country and there is a large market for raw materials and knapping tools. Knapping itself has reached new heights with the manufacture of exotics, eccentrics and replication of hearts and animals for jewellery. Some of the exotic shapes are of mystical animals and follow some of the decorated pieces from South America. The general level of craftsmanship is high and rivals anything else in the world past or present.

To give a flavour of the American scene, I asked an associate of mine, D.C. Waldorf, to draft a few words about his involvement with knapping in the States. 'DC' was one of the first people to get involved in modern American knapping and was instrumental in getting many people started on this course.

MODERN FLINT KNAPPING IN AMERICA
By D.C. Waldorf

With the exception of the few who hunt using points they made, flint knapping in America has become more of a popular hobby and art form than a useful craft. Today it has many practitioners; however, it wasn't always that way.

Back in the 1960s, when I began to experiment with flint working, I was pretty much alone. I was one of only two knappers in my home state of Ohio, and at 18, I felt that I was the better one! If there were others, they were not demonstrating their skills in the open. At that time the available information was scarce to nonexistent. The Indian relic collector society that I belonged to was totally against flint knapping because of the problem with fakes being sold, therefore they published nothing that would be of any help. On the other hand, modern academic experimenters were just getting started, with their findings being published in obscure journals that the general public had little access to, let alone understood.

To get a movement such as modern flint knapping going there had to be a spark and I believe there were actually two: one being the academic community's acceptance of the craft as a legitimate research tool and the teaching of it in special classes, and the other being the availability of a practical manual that explained the nuts and bolts in plain language.

Don Crabtree's knapping demonstrations for interested American archaeologists were legendary as was François Bordes in Europe and I believe, as do others, that my book *The Art of Flint Knapping* was the manual. I published the first edition in 1975 and it is now in its fifth edition with about 80,000 copies being sold to date. These were distributed at black powder shoots, pow-wows and historic events, through craft supply houses, museum gift shops, and they were also being used as textbooks for college courses! Though other books on knapping have been published since, *The Art of Flint Knapping*, I am pleased to say, is still considered one of the best.

Along with books came magazines, the *Flint Knappers Exchange* newsletter being the first. Although it was semi-academic in nature and was only in print from 1978 to 1981, it set the tone for others that followed with tips and articles on knapping techniques, knap-in announcements and reports on who was there, and what happened. The best and longest lived magazine that came after the *Exchange* was CHIPS. My late wife and I started this quarterly in 1989, it remained continuously in print until 2011, and I believe it was the engine that drove knapping to the position it is in today.

Before the Internet came into its own, at its peak *CHIPS* had nearly 1,200 subscribers and was the main source of current news, articles, knap-in announcements, and advertisements for supplies. As it stands now, there are no flint knapping magazines in print with the Internet providing some information, however, the four volumes of *The Best of CHIPS* and some back issues still remain available for those serious students of the craft.

With the advent of home video in the mid-1980s, it was almost no surprise that this medium would be pressed into service as a teaching tool for flint knapping, and there were some old 16mm films made of Crabtree and Bordes that were transferred to VHS and were available to a limited audience.

In 1993, the wife and I made The Art of Flint Knapping Video Companion. With the action being linked to the chapters and illustrations in the book, it was the first really practical production that set the standard and the tone for others that followed. Re-edited and transferred to DVD it's still available, along with many others on the market. Also, there are some videos now being posted on the Internet. However, even the best videos do not provide the two-way interaction that one finds at a knap-in.

As you can see, the availability of information and the advent of knap-ins has gone a long way towards taking the craft out of the hands of secretive fakers and archaeologist-experimenters, while presenting it to the general public in a more palatable form. The ranks of modern knappers have swelled due to these things and so has the number of knap-ins and attendance at meets. At present, we have about thirty knap-ins held each year around the US with the largest boasting as many as 200 participants, not including the throngs of visitors that can be in the thousands!

The face-to-face interaction between novice and advanced craftsmen has made learning easier and much faster than when we worked in isolation from one another. For example, I have a 14-year-old apprentice who, in six months, is making small arrow points on a level that took me six years to achieve on my own! With this head start advantage he could be making Danish daggers by the time he is 18! This, along with some competition, either with oneself, or with others, has driven flint knapping to the level at which it is being practiced today. We are now making works of art that, in many cases, far surpass the prehistoric prototypes to a point that they would either be greatly admired by their original makers, or would be barely recognisable to them.

On the down side, knapping can be addictive! For some the challenges are taken seriously and when successful there is just enough reward to keep them hooked. This may cause some neglect of work and family in favour of chipping! Also, there is a lot of good rock, that is a finite resource, which is being destroyed by unsupervised beginners and the advanced alike. And we are still the source of contemporary relics that can be confused with the originals. However, there are new methods of detection that have been recently developed that will eventually negate this. In the case of the craftsman who permanently marks his creations, he will be the winner, for his will stand out from the background of un-signed fakes and will be recognised for the true individual works of art that they are.

All in all, I see flint knapping in the US as a self-sustaining, growing, and evolving craft, one that has its roots in old traditions, but is not afraid to create new forms and develop new tools and techniques to get the job done. While there are still a few of us who keep the old ways alive, copper tools have replaced those of stone and antler; with rock saws and grinders being used to save material, and as aids in producing near perfect flake scar patterns. Since there are no formal flint knapping organisations keeping track of members, it is hard to even estimate how many active knappers there are. The best guesses place the number between 1,500 and 3,000. I think there may be more. All I know is back in 1975, when I went into the business full-time, virtually no one knew what a flint knapper was. Now, about 10 per cent of the people I meet on the street have heard of the craft, have seen someone demonstrate it, or personally know someone who is into it. What a difference from just 35 years ago! We have come a long way, but we still have far to go.

Author's note: DC is still one of the leading lights in American knapping (and yes we all call him DC) and in his own right is a superb knapper. I am very lucky to own one of his pieces. His late wife, Val, was also extremely talented and produced the most wonderful illustrations. I am very pleased to be able to reproduce some examples of Val's work later in this book. Val has left us an amazing legacy.

17

UK Flint Mines and USA Flint Mines

To understand Britain's need to mine flint, we first have to look at how flint was formed. The chalk as it formed had a top layer some 8m to 9m thick of detritus material of rotting corpses of sea creatures and decaying seaweed. This created hydrogen sulphide that has the ability to have an ion exchange with silicon making silicon dioxide. Through this layer filtrated SiO_2, silicon dioxide, settled into cavities and water table levels to become, over time, the flint layers we see today.

Most of the better flint used in the Stone Age was formed in the bottom part of the upper chalk and can be seen as bands of flint in places like Brighton Marina in East Sussex. The upper layer of flint within the chalk was called the 'top stone' and was the least filtered, so it is full of fossils. Lower down in the chalk are subsequent layers termed 'wall stone' and at the bottom the best flint layer 'floor stone'. For knapping, this is the flint that is most desirable, as it is usually black and very pure. In earlier chapters we saw how material in flint will deflect the shock wave so the finer and purer quality the flint, the easier it is to knap.

It was this floor stone that the Neolithic miners sought and later attracted the gun flint knappers of Norfolk in and around the Brandon area. Where this floor stone seam outcropped in the chalk, chambers were dug into the face of the chalk to recover it. Chalk is not the most reliable rock to dig into and galleries can only go so far before they tend to collapse. Soon, all the exposed seams were dug out and the only way to recover more flint was to mine it. Shafts, sometimes 10m or 12m deep, were dug until the floor stone was reached and then side galleries were worked. As galleries could only be dug so far before collapsing and abandonment, new shafts were then mined and the process repeated. This resulted in the land above ground becoming cratered, as seen at Grime's Graves in Norfolk.

There are flint mines wherever there is better quality flint, especially along the South Downs in Sussex. The Neolithic mines at Cissbury, Church Hill, Harrow Hill and Blackpatch each had a considerable number of shafts that

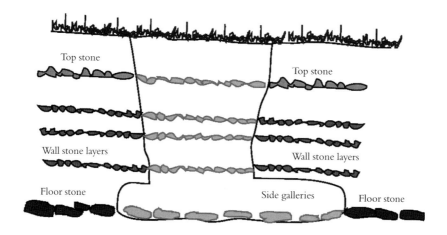

Neolithic flint mine.

now appear as shallow depressions in the ground. Large tracts of the South Downs were turned over to agriculture during the Second World War and many of these mine depressions were ploughed out.

Other parts of Europe also have prehistoric flint mines, particularly Spiennes in Belgium and also Poland, France, Spain and Germany.

In America, 'flint' was mined extensively in the past, although the shafts were not as deep as those in chalk. In Texas, near the town of Fritch, there is a mined area called the Alibates Quarries, where hundreds of pits were excavated to remove flint.

A local archaeologist, Bob Wishoff, has been working in these quarries and writes the following:

In the Panhandle region of Texas is a huge quarry area where Alibates chert, a colourful and unique form of silicified or agatised dolomite, was mined. All that is left of the quarrying activities are shallow depressions that cover over a thousand acres. Outcrops of chert cap the bluff; there are occasional boulders of red and white weathered chert, and millions of chips and chunks of multi-coloured chert debitage cover the ground.

First mentioned by Lt J.W. Abert in 1845, it remained for Charles N. Gould in 1917 to name the white dolomite 'Alibates' after nearby Alibates Creek. However, in a speech dedicating an official Texas State Historical Marker in honour of Gould, H.E. Hertner claimed that the name of Alibates flint was a corruption of the name of 'Allen Bates', a local rancher's son on whose land Alibates Creek is located. Alibates chert comprises an upper bed of dolomite, followed by a red–bed sequence, followed by a lower dolomite bed, comparable to Day Creek Oklahoma dolomite.

It is found in many colours: red, white, blue and yellow specimens are common, with green being the rarest form. Some of the best-known examples have been referred to as looking like red meat, or 'streaky bacon'.

Alibates 'flints' are among the most ubiquitous materials reported in archaeological literature and have greater distribution temporally, culturally and geographically than any other lithic material in North America. Until recently, there was no agreed upon description of Alibates chert. One suggested origin for most of the chert attributes chertification of the dolomite to secondary replacement from the silica-rich Ogallala as a by-product of the calcification process.

Alibates dolomite was a resource exploited by many peoples over a vast period of time. However, it remained for a group known as Antelope Creek culture to organise mining activities at what is now known as Alibates Flint Quarries National Monument (in Fritch, Texas). Prevailing thinking about the Antelope Creek peoples is that they used the quarries to create a 'blank-making' industry, and that those blanks were exchanged throughout the south-west, and 'down-the-line' to locations as diverse as the Pacific Coast and Minnesota. The quarries were apparently abandoned sometime in the late thirteenth century. By the time Coronado reached the area in the six-teenth century, the local inhabitants had no idea who had originally built the many occupations that surround the quarry area.

Near Fritch in Texas, this is the famous Alibates Quarries. Mined extensively for knappable quality stone, this area is currently undergoing archaeological evaluation and research by postgraduate archaeologist Bob Wishoff.

Where igneous rocks are extracted, mining tends to be more in the way of surface collection, as their volcanic origin tends to make the deposits very large.

All mines, however, have one thing in common and that is the extraction process results in large boulders and nodules that are extremely heavy. In the past, to reduce the weight of the raw material before transportation and to test the quality of the flint, rough-outs were produced. This means that all mines and quarries are also a source of the resultant waste material or debitage.

18

LET'S MAKE AN AMERICAN POINT

Everyone who starts to make American points looks at the Clovis. It is possibly the most famous of all the points but you may well have selected a different one, so let us get started.

There are several ways to accomplish the task. Firstly, working from a nodule:

1 Percussion knapping
2 Percussion knapping and pressure flaking
3 Percussion knapping, grinding and pressure flaking
4 Finishing (notching/edging/fluting)

If you are working from a pre-cut slab, then there are further choices:

1 Percussion knapping
2 Percussion knapping and pressure flaking
3 Percussion knapping, grinding and pressure flaking
4 Pressure flaking
5 Pressure flaking, grinding and further pressure flaking
6 Finishing (notching/edging/fluting)

You are therefore faced with a number of ways to work your point, so let us take each of them in turn and review the method.

Nodule Working Percussion

We have spent a large amount of time looking at the process of reducing a nodule to a thin biface. We can recap this, firstly by quartering to produce a roughly parallel-sided spall and then further reduction by thinning. It is worth restating that when you start to produce a thinner workpiece you must always remove mass from the ends rather than work the middle section. End shock is very easy at this stage, as the thinnest part of the piece is the weakest, so invariably if you reduce the wrong part in the wrong order, many hours of work can be wasted.

Remember all the lessons about thinning and reducing the platform below the centre line and to abrade the platform before each strike. The slower you work in the final stages of thinning the more likely you are to succeed. What you are trying to achieve is the correct elliptical shape and reduce the thickness/width ratio as far as possible. The thickness/width ratio will vary from point to point, as some types are not so wide as others.

You might well use percussion only to make your point and this is entirely acceptable. The shape of the point will have been your strategy from the outset but now, in the final stages, edge reduction will play a part to make your point asymmetric and to produce an aesthetically pleasing shape. Nibbling with your percussor to remove abrupt flakes will assist in reshaping but be careful that the abrupt scars are not too pronounced, as further thinning may be necessary. It is far better to reshape as you progress rather than leave the shaping to the last moment.

Percussion Knapping and Pressure Flaking

When you have reduced your point to its required thickness by percussion only, then the tool is complete but if you wish to take the process a little further, then you have to prepare the piece for further reduction by pressure flaking. The regular flaking that can be achieved by this method is, for most people, far more pleasing to the eye, as it does reduce all of the small inconsistencies of percussion.

If you want to put a further surface on your point, then the edge must be prepared so that you have platforms for the pressure flaker to grasp on to. Usually this can be done by heavy grinding of the edge that will not result in much loss of width. The grinding must be of sufficient magnitude to give space for the pressure flaker and also give enough strength to the platform for the flaker to work. Insufficient strength of the platform will only result in crushing the edge, so this means working slowly and carefully. There is a tendency to rush ahead in the final stages, as completion is not far away, but remember, this is when your point is most vulnerable to breaking.

If you want to pressure flake one side of the point at a time, grind the continuous platform and, working towards you, work one side of the length of the point. You will find the pressure flaking will be slightly angled, so when you rotate the point to work the second edge, the flakes will align. When one side is complete then the process of platform preparation starts all over again. Repeat the process for the other side, duplicating all the stages of the first side.

Flaking over Grinding

Another way of completing your point is by a process known as FOG (flaking over grinding). At the completion of the percussion stage, the whole surface of the point is ground in the same way as a polished axe is made. This can be a hand process, where the point is rubbed on to a grinding table, or it can be done with a bench grinder, the choice is yours. The act of grinding will produce a flat, curved surface on both sides of your point that makes pressure flaking far easier. Remember, however, that every part of the ground surface must be removed by pressure flaking, so there must be a sufficient platform to enable pressure flakes to travel more than halfway across the point. Nothing looks worse than a flaked piece with patches of grinding still showing down the centre.

The flaking is exactly the same as the directly onto percussion flaking, but due to the fact that you are working on a far more even surface the flaking can, if done well, be superb.

Finishing (Notching/Edging/Fluting)

The process of notching has been covered in earlier chapters but we can look at some additional hints. Many American knappers use horseshoe nails for small entry notching, as they are very strong and quite thin so there is less chance of breaking the point of a tapering copper pressure flaker. A case hardened awl can be used but care must be taken when using steel; there is always a firm gripping point, as similar metals tend to slide off flints. The fact that most notching is done with vertical pressure will assist, but care must be taken if the tool is being used at a shallower angle.

If the piece being worked is too thick because it has been insufficiently thinned, then notching becomes very difficult. Every time you take off any kind of spall, this involves shock waves, so again, slow steps with care are the order of the day. Be aware that if your thinning has not produced the correct elliptical shape and the point is too thick in the middle, then notching becomes almost impossible.

Some points have a serrated edge and this can be achieved by taking tiny flakes from one side of the piece with a very pointed flaker. Also, the edge of a point can be sharpened by a final pass of delicate flaking that is slightly abrupt but does not progress too far into the workpiece.

If you are making a Clovis or Folsom point the last stage is fluting. Let me say here and now, this is the most difficult part of knapping to get a flake to run a considerable way into the point at right angles to the knapping or pressure flaking. To do this requires detailed preparation for the platform and a steady nerve, hand and eye to take the flake off. Nothing is more likely to snap your point than removing a flute. The removal of the first flute is difficult enough but then you have to reverse the point and take a similar flute from the other side. Trust me, you have to be a master knapper to do this, as you may have spent hours and hours preparing your point to this stage only to break it at the very last moment.

To take a successful flute, the base of the point has to be concave, leaving a tiny nipple from where the flute will flow. As the base is made concave, the centre is left to form a small platform and this can then be struck by hand, as it was done in antiquity, or by the use of a jig developed by today's knappers. The jig works on the principle of a fulcrum and a long lever that allows a build up of pressure to be constant until the flint flake gives way. To find out more about jigs, as there are many different designs, the Internet is a valuable source of information.

19

FURTHER KNAPPING TECHNIQUES (HEAT-TREATING)

Many of the knappable rocks can be made easier to work by heat-treating. There is some speculation that flint in prehistoric Britain was treated in this way but the present evidence is inconclusive. Modern flint knappers, however, have developed methods of heat-treating many knappable materials.

There are three main ways to heat-treat rock, from cheap to expensive: in a fire pit, roaster oven and pottery kiln. A word of warning, however, that if you experiment with this process you must take the utmost caution, as hot rock can be dangerous, with this not always being apparent.

I must make a disclaimer here: The author can take no responsibility whatsoever if, in following this text, accidents or burns occur, so you have been warned. If in doubt wait several hours for things to cool down and never try a 'touch method', as working with high temperatures your skin will stick to the material being treated. Keep all heating fires and apparatus well away from children and animals.

Smaller pieces of knapping material heat-treat better than thicker ones, so spalls are the order of the day with nothing over 3cm to 4cm thick.

The First Method is the Fire Pit

Dig a shallow pit well away from all flammable material, plants and trees. In the bottom of the pit layer loose soil or sand and then build a fire on this surface. As well as wood, coal or charcoal will add to the heat generated. Keep the fire going for a few hours and then leave until the following day.

The next day scrape away the fire remains and the dried-out soil, piling it to the edges of the pit as it will be used again. In the bottom, layer the spalls of flint no more than two or three spalls thick and replace the scraped fire remains back over the flint. The flint must be buried by at least 3cm to 4cm of dried soil and fire material and if this is insufficient, add dry sand. Replace the fire and relight, replenishing when needed until the fire has been going for twelve hours. It is advisable to start in the morning so you are not leaving a burning fire unattended at night. When the fire has burned out, leave for at least two days, three is better. Uncover the middle of the flint layer and splash a few drops of water to ensure that the flint is cold before removing.

This method will heat the flint to about 300°C to 350°C when buried at 2½cm and then deduct 10°C for every centimetre deeper. Leaving the fire to burn for twelve hours ensures that there is uniform temperature to soak the flint.

The Oven Roaster

Roasters are available at a reasonable price from the Internet. They will not reach the higher temperatures of the fire pit, yet will give a great deal more control over temperature. Removal of the inner liner can assist in creating a higher temperature but beware, as this makes the exterior very hot so again be warned about keeping children and animals away.

At higher temperatures, the inside of the Roaster does not give a uniform heat, as the corners and the bottom of the Roaster will always be hot spots. The way to use the Roaster is to bury the spalls upright in a sand or vermiculite layer to ensure that the spalls do not touch each other. Set the temperature at 100°C for a few hours to dry out the flint and then increase the temperature slowly by 10°C intervals until the required temperature is achieved or the Roaster is at maximum. It is crucial to ensure that your flint is really dry, as water pockets can blow out at higher temperatures.

When the flint has soaked for a few hours, reduce the temperature incrementally the same as for the heating process and when it has reduced to 100°C, switch off the Roaster and leave it for at least a day.

The Pottery Kiln

This is by far the best way to heat-treat but it is also the most expensive. A kiln is a large cash outlay but it does give you complete control of the temperature at all stages of the process. Again you need to dry out your rock and, if using the higher final temperature, leave at 100°C for up to seven or eight hours. The best thing is to operate the kiln overnight. Follow the same procedure as the Roaster but do not fall into the trap of having a 'sneak peek' to see if all is going well. The kiln should be left for at least two days after switching off.

The following is an indication of materials and times:

British flint: 200°C to 250°C for 6 to 8 hours
Chalcedony: 280°C to 320°C for 2 to 4 hours
Agate: 200°C to 240°C for 1 to 2 hours
Kaolin: 160°C to 180°C for 4 to 6 hours
Petrified wood: 180°C to 280°C for 2 to 4 hours
Novaculite: 410°C to 490°C for 4 to 6 hours
Chert: 320°C to 350°C for 3 to 4 hours
Jasper: 260°C to 320°C for 5 to 6 hours

These times are only approximate, as there is no substitute for experimentation. Also, especially with rocks like chert or chalcedony, there can be a great variation in quality, which means that it will affect the timing and the temperature.

You can also acquire heat-treated rock from the Internet, so I would suggest you try knapping with this first, as well as untreated, to see the difference before making your own. Heat-treated material reacts differently to untreated and will affect the way you knap.

20

SUMMING IT ALL UP

I f you have worked your way through this book, by now you should be an accomplished knapper, but if you have skipped to this bit or are just reading through, then let us recap on some of the major mistakes that can be made but also tips for success.

Firstly, and far and away the most important … slow down. The biggest mistake people make is to proceed too quickly. Each time you hit a rock you produce a shock wave, so there is little point in hitting over and over again, as all you are doing is fragmenting the rock. The expert knapper will invariably, after a strike, pause, examine, abrade, sum up the next strike and align the workpiece and hammer and then, and only then, make the next strike. In this instance, it is much like a golf professional who checks the lie of the course, looks and assesses the distance, takes a few practice swings and then plays the ball.

With knapping you cannot have a second chance. Make a mistake and you have a fault that may be impossible to recover from. Many master knappers spend considerable time preparing the platform and can take minutes, not seconds, between strikes. So if you rush it you are on the path to spoiling it.

Learn to select your rock, take a hammer stone or a bopper with you and sample the rock – you could even trim down to a spall or a rough-out to save carrying away lots of unwanted weight. The recognition of knappable quality comes with experience, so assess and test your rocks. In fact, take great care, as selection is the first stage of knapping.

When quartering, remember that the shock wave will always take the path of least resistance. This is also the rule if you do not put enough force into your strike, as the shock wave runs out of energy and hinges rather than feathers. Also remember that cortex is a very bad conductor of shock waves, so you have to make the easiest strike to create the first real platform on the inside of the rock. This means that your hammer stone or hammer must be big enough and heavy enough to do the job required. Reacquaint yourself with the Hertzian cone angle of 100 degrees, so you get the correct strike angle and the best use of your nodule.

The strike to create a perfect spall or a perfect flake depends on five elements:

1   The angle of the strike hammer
2   The angle of the workpiece
3   How the piece is supported
4   The strike angle itself
5   The force of the blow

All of these elements have to be taken into account but remember it takes time to get everything running smoothly. It is rather like learning to drive a car, when you pushed the pedals for the clutch and accelerator and turned the steering wheel but then forgot to check the mirror. It takes time to get most of these things in the right order so that it becomes automatic. Knapping is the same and it too will become automatic with practice. You must be able to achieve the ability to hit in the right place and with the correct part of your hammer. It can take a while to learn how to control your muscles to do this.

When working your flint, ensure that the platform is always below the centre line of the spall and remember the importance of abrading. If your platform is not substantial enough to carry the shock wave it will crush, so, if in doubt, abrade again. Thinning flakes always need to be heavily abraded, as you want them to carry at least further than the centre of the workpiece, otherwise they are not thinning.

One of the main mistakes is not thinking through the shape of your tool as a triangular cross section, which is a very common occurrence. We have said that the way you hit and from which side you hit may well be counter-intuitive, so review the section of thinning. Remember to thin the ends of a workpiece before you tackle the middle, as this can be a great way to end up with two smaller workpieces! You must be able to 'see' the finished tool inside the nodule at all stages of knapping.

Practice over and over again the removal of parallel-sided blades from a Mousterian core, as blade removal develops your ability far quicker than any other knapping task.

When you start knapping, there is so much to think about that you will most certainly make a lot of rubble as you turn rocks into gravel, but keep going, as all knappers have had to go through this learning stage.

With pressure flaking, remember that it is the angle of attack that counts. If your flakes are short, you are flaking at an incorrect angle. Practise on glass as it's the cheapest material you can find. You need something thicker than window glass but your local glazier should have something and can cut it into 4cm or 5cm strips for you. My local glazier had a broken coffee table top that he had just replaced and was delighted to find someone who would pay money for what to him was scrap. I bought enough glass strips to last me five months, all for the princely sum of £10. Your pressure flakes on glass should be at least 3cm so if you are falling short, adjust your knapping angles.

Make sure you have a selection of tools, hammer stones or boppers, ishi sticks and pressure flakers. Make sure you have a glove that fits your supporting hand to avoid cuts (a golfing glove is great). You can add tape to the fingers of your glove to give added protection. Get a proper knee pad, old carpet is good, a rubberised bath mat works well, but leather is best (yet can be expensive).

Lastly but most importantly, be proud of your achievements. Keep what you make and show it around; you will be amazed how people respond to flint tools, even your first attempts. After a while you will look back over your earlier work and either throw it away or more often rework your first tries. Knapping is a wonderful art form and gives great pleasure as your ability to create improves.

You are recreating the past and coming closer to those long-lost ancestors who made their tools and depended on flint for their livelihood. Good luck in your endeavours to become a flint knapper and may you get as much enjoyment from this as I have done!

21

ILLUSTRATING YOUR FLINTS

When you have built up a collection of your work, it is always nice to have a portfolio of what you have achieved. You will find that photographs are not always the best way to see all the nuances of your working, as the many facets of the flint are notoriously difficult to photograph. A good way to keep a record is to draw your finished flints. As well as being a lot of fun to do, there is an added bonus as it makes you really look at your work. The act of drawing enables you to see more of what you have accomplished and shows your errors in stark relief!

I assure you that by drawing your flints you will learn more than you ever thought you would. This is because you are looking in great detail at every facet of the flint. Whether you can draw or not, try it as it is well worth the exercise. As an illustrator teaching how to draw artefacts, I am always being told, 'but I have no artistic ability' and to this I say, 'great'. An illustrator is someone who puts on paper exactly what they see and nothing more. Teaching people with artistic talent is usually very difficult, as they always want to enhance and interpret the drawing and they are the very things you do not need.

Let's look at some illustrations, especially those by Val Waldorf.

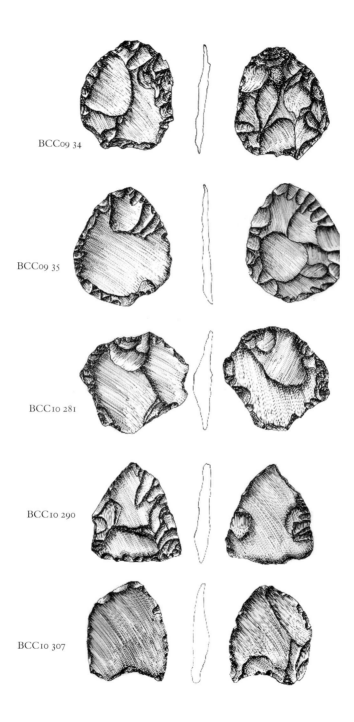

BCC09 34

BCC09 35

BCC10 281

BCC10 290

BCC10 307

Drawn by the author.

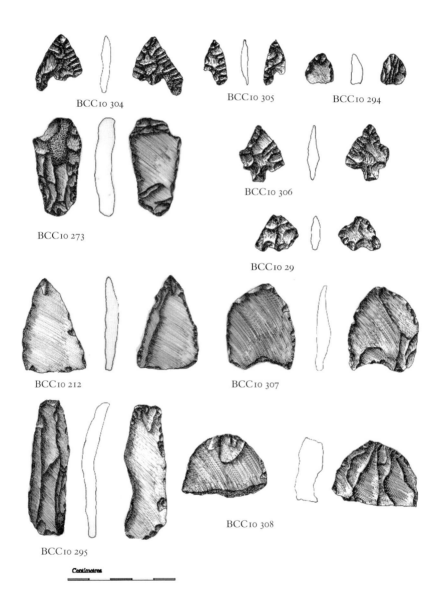

BCC10 304

BCC10 305

BCC10 294

BCC10 273

BCC10 306

BCC10 29

BCC10 212

BCC10 307

BCC10 295

BCC10 308

Centimetres

Drawn by the author.

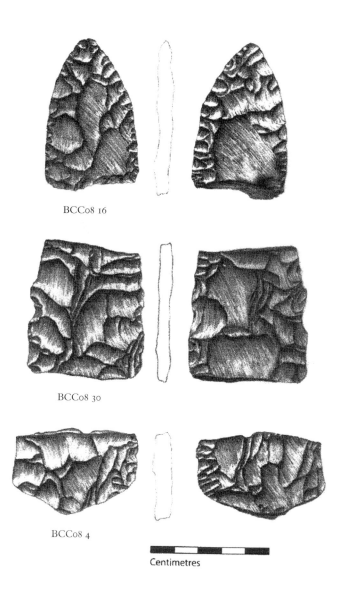

BCC08 16

BCC08 30

BCC08 4

Centimetres

Beaker period dagger fragments (drawn by the author).

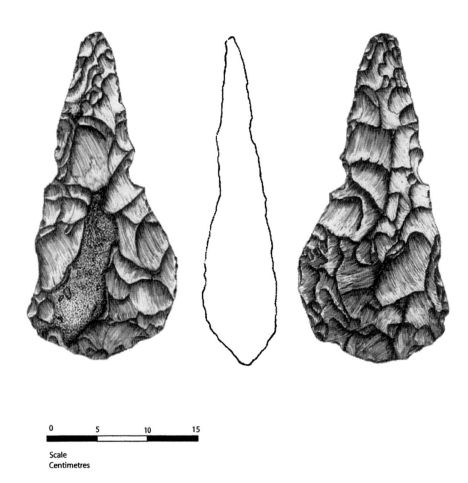

0   5   10   15

Scale
Centimetres

Lower Palaeolithic ficron biface hand axe (drawn by the author).

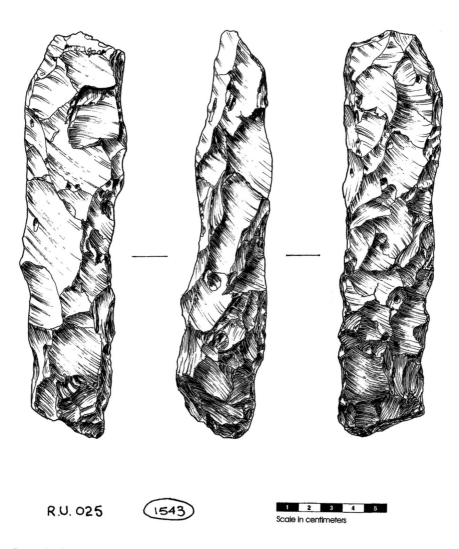

R.U. 025   (1543)   Scale in centimeters
1 2 3 4 5

Drawn by the author.

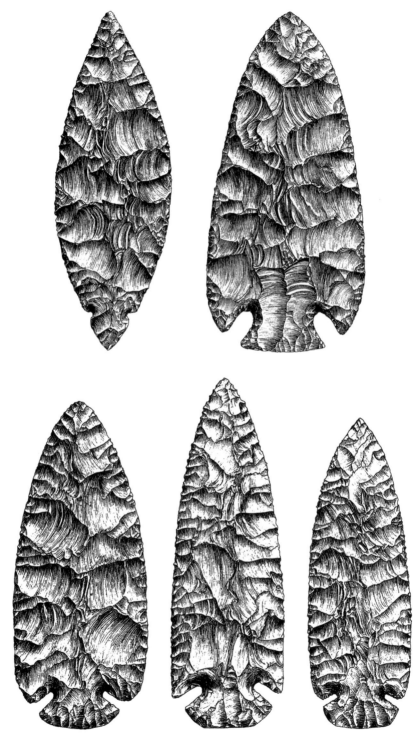

By Val Waldorf.

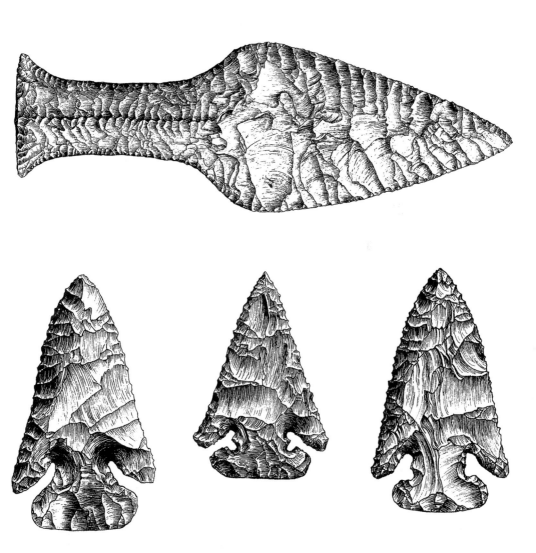

By Val Waldorf.

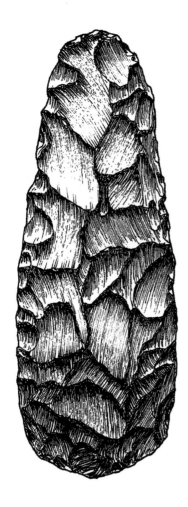
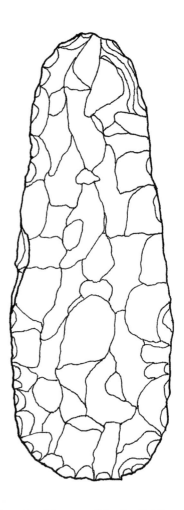

Two sides of a biface; one complete, the other half drawn. An illustration of the stages of drawing: first the outline and the flake scars, then complete the drawing. By the author.

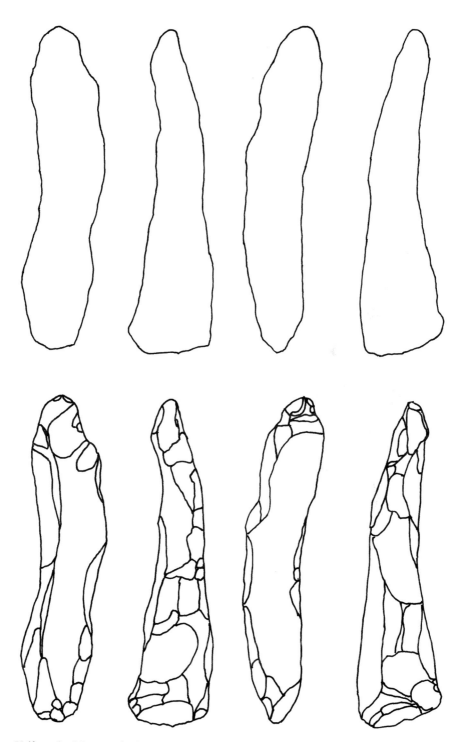

Half-completed drawings (by the author).

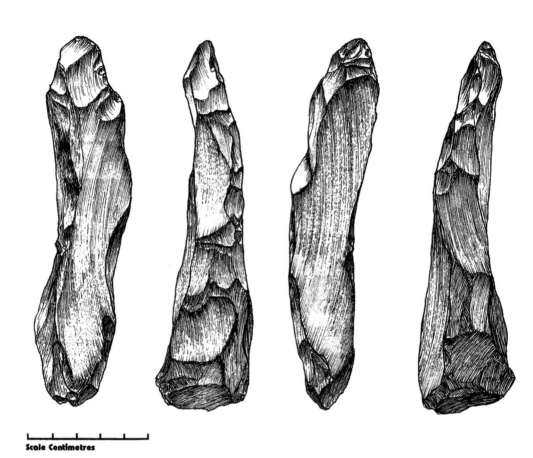

Scale Centimetres

Final drawing of the pick (drawn by the author).

So how do you go about drawing flints? To start with, flints are usually drawn at four times their full size, so when the finished flint is drawn, it is reduced back to normal size and looks much better as minor blemishes are hidden.

Starting with the outline, this must be as accurate as possible, so the easiest way is to scan the flint into your computer. Scan into a drawing programme that allows you to double the linear scale by two. (If you do not have a drawing programme, you can obtain a free copy of 'Serif DrawPlus – Starter Addition' from the Internet as a download. This will do everything you want for a basic drawing programme, which is all you require for simple outline illustration.)

When you have scanned the flint, using your drawing programme, print off the image and you are now ready to transfer this to your drawing paper or film. Archaeological drawing is usually done on a medium called 'permatrace', that is an inert transparent film that does not expand or contract. If you are using permatrace then all you need to do is place it over your scan printout and trace round the edge. If you are using paper, with a soft 2B or 4B pencil, cover the back of the scan print with a layer of graphite and then place it on top of your paper and trace round the flint edges. This gives you an outline that is very accurate.

Holding the flint next to your drawing, lightly draw in the flint scar facets. Do this in pencil so you can erase errors as you go along. Comparing the original flint alongside the drawing enables you to get facets in the correct position, especially those facets that reach the edge of the flint. The idea is to get as accurate a representation of the flint as possible.

Having now created an outline of your flint you need to switch to pen and ink. You need proper drafting pens that can be obtained from any good art shop. Nibs usually come in sizes 0.25, 0.32, 0.5 and 0.7. Using a thick nib (I usually do this at 0.5) trace the outside edge of the flint, then, using a lesser nib (I usually use 0.25), trace in all the facets. Wait until the ink is dry and then erase all pencil marks so only the ink is left. The drawing is now ready to finish.

If you wish to make your drawing look professional, this can be done at any stage by using your scanner and doubling the linear size. This makes the image four times larger than the original. Print this off and follow the same sequence as above.

The facet markings are not, repeat not, shading. They are a representation of the ripples within the facet, so you have to look carefully at your flint to see which way the facet was struck. The standard convention of flint drawing is that light comes in from the top left, so the left-hand side is always lighter than the right, which makes your drawing look real.

The ripple marks are put in using a 0.25 pen. A word of warning is that drawing pen nibs are quite delicate so do not press too hard or be rough otherwise you can break the nib.

If you are drawing at x4, when your drawing is complete, scan it and reduce the linear scale by half and this will put the flint back to its original size.

Have fun and, like everything else in knapping, you will get better with practice.

BIBLIOGRAPHY

Bordaz, J., *Tools of the Old and New Stone Age* (David and Charles Ltd, 1971)

Butler, C., *Prehistoric Flintwork* (The History Press, 2005)

Forrest, A.J., *Masters of Flint* (Terence Dalton Ltd, 1983)

Justice, N.D. & Kudlaty, S.K., *Field Guide to Projectile Points of the Midwest* (Indiana University Press, 2001)

LaBudde, B.F. & Melvin, M., *Angel Mounds: A Mississippian Town on the Ohio River* (Friends of Angel Mounds, 2011)

Oakley, K.P., *Man the Tool-maker, Bulletin of the British Museum (Natural History), 1949* (The British Museum, 1972)

Stanford, D.J. & Bradley, B.A., *Across Atlantic Ice* (University of California Press, 2012)

Waldorf, D.C., *The Art of Flint Knapping* (Mound Builders Books, 1975)

Glossary of Terms

Abrader – Rough stone for abrading, usually part of a grind wheel or mill-stone grit

Abrading – Removing or rubbing down a sharp edge to make the platform stronger

Abrupt retouch – Short flake scars struck at an obtuse angle

Adze – Core tool with a transverse sharp edge used for woodworking

Awl – Pointed tool used for hole making abruptly retouched along one side or two alternate edges

Backed knife – Blade where back edge retains cortex and front edge is sharp

Barb – Side arms on an arrowhead

Barbed and tanged arrowhead – Arrowhead with a tail and side arms

Biface – Core tool of lenticular shape

Blade – A flake whose length is more than twice its width

Bladelets – A flake whose length is more than twice its width but is less than 12mm wide

Bopper – Name given to a hard hammer usually made of solid copper or copper shell filled with lead

Borer – See piercer

Boxgrove – Early site in Sussex for Heidelbergensis

Bronze Age – 2,600 BC to 700 BC

Bulb of percussion – The raised portion of a flake next to the point of impact. The first wave of the shock wave

Burin – Engraving tool made from a blade with spalls removed from the distal end to make a 90-degree square edge

Chalcedony – Rock in the silica group of materials

Chalk – 98 per cent pure calcium carbonate

Chert – Silicon dioxide deposit in limestone

Chopper – Crude tool with a sharpened edge

Clovis – First classical point type found in America

Combination tool – Blade or flake that has more than one tool use (e.g. piercer and a scraper)

Conchoidal fracture – Shock wave separation in cryptocrystalline material

Cone of fracture – See Hertzian cone

Core tool – Tool produced by the reduction of a nodule

Cortex – Outer crust on flint or chert

Crested blade – Blade with a prominent ridge running the length of the dorsal side

Crested core – Core with a prominent ridge along its work face

Cryptocrystalline – No structure grain or sheer lines

Dacite – Metamorphic rock suitable for knapping

Daggers – Flint tools made to replicate metal daggers

Dance blades – Extremely large blades made in America for ritual purposes

Debitage – Waste material during the knapping process

Denticulate – Serrated edged blade

Devensian Ice Age – Last ice age relented 12,000 years ago

Discoidal knife – Circular knife with a sharp edge sometimes with 360 degrees of sharpening

Distal end – The tip of a flake

Dorsal side – The side of a flake that was outside the core when struck

Drill – Pointed tool used for hole making abruptly retouched along parallel sides

End scraped – Blade or flake that has abrupt retouch on the distal end

End shock – When a shock wave causes a fracture in another place separate from the point of contact and breaks the nodule into two pieces

Fabricator – Elongated triangular or D-shaped cross section tool that may have been used as a pressure flaker

Feathered flake – Perfect amount of force and the flake terminates with a very thin cross section

Flake tool – Tool made from a primary flake

Flint – Silicon dioxide SiO_2 found in chalk and a collective term for knappable rocks

Floor stone – In a flint deposit the bottom layer of flint

Fluting – Removal of an elongated flake taken from one or both sides of a point to allow for hafting

Folsom – Very early American point type

Granite – Metamorphic rock suitable for knapping

Gun flint – Firing mechanism on flintlock guns where flint creates sparks against high carbon steel

Hammer stone – Spherical stone used as a flake removing percussion tool

Hand axe – Lenticular-shaped core tool used for chopping

Happisburg (pronounced Hays-boro) – One of the earliest sites in Norfolk dating back to Homo Erectus or Homo Antecessor

Hertzian cone – The 100-degree cone of shattering emanating from the point of percussion

Hinge fracture – When a shock wave runs out of energy and comes out of the core sideways leaving a rounded end

Interglacial – Warm periods between ice ages

Interstadial – Brief warm period during an ice age

Invasive retouch – Long flake scars struck at an oblique angle

Ishi stick – Long-handled pressure flaker named after its inventor

Knapping – The ability to sever spalls from cryptocrystalline rocks in the direction intended

Knife – Blade with a sharp edge

Lanceolate blade – Long, thin worked blade tapering to a point at one or both ends

Leaf point – Arrowhead made in the shape of a laurel leaf

Levallois – A technique of reducing a nodule by creating a dome and striking it off to make a biconvex spall

Limestone – Any sedimentary rock consisting essentially of carbonates

Livre de Beurre (pound of butter) – Name given to an elongated Levallois core that produces long blades

Medial – The middle portion of a flake

Mesolithic – 10,000 BP to 5,400 BP

Microlith – Retouched broken-down pieces of bladelets used to make a multi-bladed tool like a sickle

Neolithic – 4,000 BC to 2,600 BC

Notched flake – Blade or flake that has a worked notch made with abrupt retouch

Novaculite – Metamorphic rock suitable for knapping

Obsidian – Volcanic glass

Ovate – Biconvex biface narrowing at the lesser diameter end

Overshoot flakes – Caused by too much force and flake tries to continue round the nodule

Pakefield – One of the earliest sites in Norfolk dating back to Homo Erectus or Homo Antecessor

Pick – Pointed core tool used for digging

Piercer – Pointed tool used for hole making abruptly retouched along two lateral edges

Platform – The place where a flake is struck at the point of impact

Pressure flake – Tiny flake removed by hand-held pressure flaker

Pressure flaker – Tool used in the hand to increase pressure until the workpiece gives way and releases a flake

Proximal end – The base of a flake from where it was struck

Quartering – Reduction of a raw nodule into suitable spalls

Ridges – The raised boundary between flakes

Rhyolites – Glassy acid volcanic rock

Sedimentary – Geologic deposit of material over time

Sharpening flake – Tiny flake removed to re-sharpen an axe

Side scraper – Blade or flake that has abrupt retouch along one edge

Silicon – Element number 14 on the periodic table

Soft hammer – Antler or wooden hammer

Spall – First removal from a nodule that is suitable for further knapping

Step fracture – When a shock wave hits something that impedes its progress and abruptly terminates

Stone Age – Period from the first 'man' to circa 11,000 years ago

Tang – Tail on an arrowhead

Thickness ratio – Comparing width to thickness to give a measure of how 'thin' a tool is

Thinning flake – Very thin flakes removed to reduce the thickness of the tool being made

Top stone – In a flint deposit the upper layer of flint

Tranchet flake – Tiny flake removed to re-sharpen an axe taken transversely across the tool

Undershoot flakes – Caused by insufficient force and will hinge fracture out of the core

Upper Palaeolithic – Last period of the Palaeolithic 40,000 to 15,000 years ago

Ventral side – The side of a flake that was inside the core when struck

Wall stone – In a flint deposit the intermediate layers of flint

Y scraper – Scraper made on the convex end of a flake to produce a Y shape

INDEX

The author of this book, aged 69 at the time of writing, lives in West Sussex and is a member of the Lithics
Society, the Sussex Archaeological Society, Worthing, Brighton and Hove Societies and is a knapping tutor
at Sussex University, Butser Iron Age Village and Amberley Open Air Museum. He is also a tutor in
archaeological illustration and an associate member of the Institute of Field Archaeology with ten years'
experience in knapping.

If you enjoyed this book, you may also be interested in…

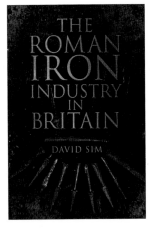

The Roman Iron Industry in Britain

DAVID SIM

The invasion of AD 43 began the Romans' settlement of Britain. The Romans brought with them a level of expertise that raised iron production in Britain from small localised sites to an enormous industry. Rome thrived on war and iron was vital to the Roman military establishment, as well as to the civil population. In this pioneering work, David Sim combines current ideas of iron-making in Roman times with experimental archaeology. This is a fully revised and updated edition of the author's previous co-authored *Iron for the Eagles* (The History Press 2002).

978 0 7524 6865 5

Prehistoric Rock Art in the North York Moors

PAUL BROWN & GRAEME CHAPPELL

This revised edition is an accumulation of two decades of research and fieldwork by the authors, and presents a comprehensive account of the little-known prehistoric rock art within the North York Moors area. It covers Northern England's last major area of rock art and describes the geographical and moorland setting of sites, including those associated with other archaeological monuments. Included is a new section on recording techniques using laser, photogrammetry and other methods, an updated gazetteer of recently discovered rock art sites in the North York Moors area, and appendices providing details of recent major discoveries within the area.

978 0 7524 6877 8

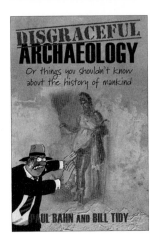

Disgraceful Archaeology Or Things You Shouldn't Know about the History of Mankind

PAUL BAHN AND BILL TIDY

The book that all archaeology buffs have secretly been yearning for! This unique blend of text, anecdote and cartoon reveals, and revels in, those aspects of the past that have been ignored, glossed over or even suppressed – the bawdy, the scatological and the downright bizarre. Our ancestors were not always serious, downtrodden and fearful creatures. They were human like ourselves and shared our earthy sense of humour that is based on bodily functions, bawdiness and slapstick. So let's take the fig leaf off the past and have a long, hard look at our true history.

978 0 7524 6596 8

Visit our website and discover thousands of other History Press books.

www.thehistorypress.co.uk